D1117584

CLOSING
THE
OPEN
DOOR

CLOSING
THE
OPEN
DOOR

American=Japanese Diplomatic Negotiations
1936=1941

JAMES H. HERZOG

Naval Institute Press
Annapolis, Maryland

Contents

Preface

The role of the United States Navy in Japanese-American relations just prior to United States entry in World War II serves as an excellent example of a military branch of one country significantly influencing its government's foreign relations with another country. For five years before the Japanese attack on Pearl Harbor, as the tempo of world affairs reached crises which resulted inevitably in war, the leadership of the United States Navy enjoyed a special position in the highest councils of the United States government unparalleled before or since. One could categorically say that it was the heyday of direct American naval influence in foreign relations. Although that influence affected Britain, the Netherlands, and Germany, it was most pronounced vis-à-vis Japan.

That naval strategic thinking was oriented towards Japan and the Pacific area should not be a surprise. In the Atlantic, only Britain of the European powers had a sizable navy and that was considered more of a complement to United States security than a threat. In the Pacific, since the United States had acquired the Philippine Islands in 1898 after a short war with Spain, the one maritime nation which could threaten United States national interests was Japan. The strategic advantage of Japan over the United States improved exponentially as a result of her opportune participation in World War I. During that war she took from Germany possession of the Caroline, Palau, Gilbert, Marianas (less Guam which was American), and Marshall island groups, and subsequently had her seizures blessed by mandate from the League of Nations. In 1922 the same naval treaty which gave Japan 60 percent parity with the fleets of Britain and the United States also stipulated that Japan would not fortify the mandated islands nor would the United States fortify any of her possessions west of Hawaii.

Almost immediately after the Naval Treaty of 1922 Japan enshrouded the mandated islands in secrecy, denying visits by foreigners who might observe whether in fact she was adhering to the provisions of non-fortification. At the opposite end of the spectrum of what could be observed, the Japanese naval units and their actions in Chinese waters were familiar sights to the officers and men of the United States Asiatic Fleet. As Britain, France, and the Netherlands, in addition to the United States and Japan, competed for their share of commerce with China, so each nation had naval ships on the China Station.

The five senior admirals who were directly involved in the United States strategy with Japan from 1936 to 1941 had each served in the Asiatic Fleet prior to becoming admiral, so each had had a previous conditioning for subsequent events. Admiral Harry E. Yarnell, as Commander in Chief, Asiatic Fleet, dealt directly with the Imperial Japanese naval commanders in China during Japan's war with China commencing in 1937. Yarnell's successor, Admiral Thomas C. Hart, continued direct relations with Japanese officials during a time when, because of the war in Europe, the only occidental naval force in China was American. Hart also tasted the gall of defeat by superior Japanese forces which smashed through the thin Allied defenses en route to rich prizes in the Netherlands East Indies in January and February of 1942. Admirals James O. Richardson and Husband E. Kimmel, as successive commanders of the U.S. Fleet, took exception to the concept of using the fleet in Hawaii to deter Japan from aggression in the Southwest Pacific. The former objected vehemently to stationing the fleet in Hawaii where he thought it could not be properly trained or supported, while the latter doggedly deplored the constant deterioration of the effectiveness of the fleet. But it was Admiral Harold R. Stark, as Chief of Naval Operations, who exerted the most powerful influence on President Franklin D. Roosevelt, Secretary of State Cordell Hull, and Army Chief of Staff George C. Marshall. Stark's strategic plan to do everything possible to assist Britain in her fight against Germany and to keep the peace in the Pacific, at almost any price, would be followed until only weeks before Japan broke the peace with the Pearl Harbor attack which brought the United States into World War II.

This book describes the roles these five admirals and their subordinates played in Japanese-American relations in the five years before the Pearl Harbor attack.

In my research one of the most fortunate aspects was the quality and quantity of original documents made available to me. Within the

Naval History Division I was allowed access to the complete files of the War Plans Division; the Chief of Naval Operations and the Secretary of the Navy files; the unpublished work of Captain Tracy Kittredge which purportedly was to have been a history of the U.S. Navy in World War II; the unpublished narrative of Admiral Thomas C. Hart; and naval orders and documents which were promulgated only within the structure of the Office of the Chief of Naval Operations. From a researcher's point of view, I found most enjoyable the meticulously indexed and cross-referenced classified State Department files in the National Archives. These Washington sources were complemented by the Roosevelt Papers at Hyde Park, records and documents in the Naval War College, and the invaluable volumes of the various investigations of the Pearl Harbor attack.

I am very grateful to a large number of persons without whose help I would never have finished this book. I am particularly appreciative for the assistance of: Lieutenant Commander Arnold S. Lott, USN (Retired) as senior book editor of the Naval Institute Press in making suggestions and for his Job-like patience; Captain F. Kent Loomis, USN, former director of naval history, for expediting my clearances to classified navy records; Commander Burton Robert Truxler, USN, for his prompt work in declassifying those selections which I desired; Dr. Dean C. Allard, of the Naval History Division for his always professional cooperation; Mrs. Patricia Dowling for cheerfully and efficiently supplying the voluminous files in the diplomatic records section of the National Archives and for promptly answering numerous subsequent queries; Dr. Whitney Trow Perkins, as my doctoral adviser at Brown University; Dean Ernest R. May, Harvard University, who encouraged me to write the book; and lastly my wife Jacqueline and daughters who made the sacrifices of their time while I wrote.

Any mistakes or shortcomings are solely mine and should not reflect upon any of my cherished acquaintances who have helped me along the way.

CLOSING
THE
OPEN
DOOR

CHAPTER 1

Tension and Frustration in the Pacific

On December 8, 1936, President Franklin Delano Roosevelt was on board the cruiser USS *Indianapolis* as she steamed north off the coast of Brazil. The President, in the comfort and security of the admiral's quarters, had relaxed on his post-election cruise, yet he was deeply concerned about recent international events.

He had just learned of the Anti-Comintern Pact of November 25, tying Japan to Germany and Italy in agreements ostensibly against communism and the Third International. Germany, the previous spring, had violated the Treaty of Versailles and the Locarno Treaties by reoccupying the demilitarized Rhineland, and the Italians had taken Addis Ababa in July to end the Ethiopian war. The actions of the two European militants seemed to be part of the pattern begun by the Japanese in their seizure of Manchuria in 1931. The news that the three leading aggressors of the time were united was certainly reason enough for the President to express concern.

Roosevelt sent for his naval aide, Captain Paul Bastedo, and asked him about the status of America's war plans. It was a pregnant question, symptomatic of the shift in focus in Roosevelt's second term, and it was not answerable by Bastedo. The aide immediately wrote a memorandum to the Chief of Naval Operations suggesting a complete analysis be given the President on the subject war plans.[1]

Exactly five years after the President queried his naval aide concerning war plans, the United States Navy would be crippled in the greatest naval disaster in American history—the highly successful Japanese attack on the United States Pacific Fleet at Pearl Harbor, Hawaii. That December "day of infamy" would presage a war during which Roosevelt would die in office and the *Indianapolis* would be the

1

last major U.S. naval vessel sunk by the Japanese. In those five years Roosevelt would ask hundreds of questions of his naval subordinates—sometimes heeding and sometimes disregarding their counsel. He would use senior naval officers as special envoys to the British and Dutch and as ambassadors to Vichy France and the Soviet Union. Naval officers would become militarily and diplomatically involved with Japanese officials in China and Washington. They would attempt to influence their counterparts in the Departments of State and War to enlist further support in winning presidential approval of naval analyses and plans.

Early in January 1937, Captain Bastedo received from the Chief of Naval Operations the answer to his memorandum requesting the status of war plans—a six-page synopsis of the war plans situation as envisioned by officers in the War Plans Division, who worked for the Chief of Naval Operations. The review of plans given Captain Bastedo covered the major contingency and supporting plans of the Navy, but emphasized the *Orange Plan,* the plan for war in the Pacific. "Practically all detailed planning [was] confined to this plan as the Joint Board had decided that war in the Pacific [was] more probable than war with any other major naval Power."[2]

The attention of senior officers of the United States Navy through 1936 into 1937 continued to be focused in the Pacific and on future relations with Japan, even though U.S. newspapers in 1936 were filled with accounts of actions by Germany and Italy and the outbreak of the Spanish Civil War. Naval strategists viewed their problems in the light of the traditional roles of the Navy in the Pacific, the theories of Captain Alfred Thayer Mahan, the history of Japanese actions in the Pacific, the restraints of the recent naval treaties, and the attitudes of the statesmen of the nation towards problems in the Orient.

The U.S. Navy's assessment of Japan as the most likely enemy of the United States had obvious historical roots. Almost every month some incident involving Americans and Japanese reinforced this apprehension. In the last six months of 1936, various incidents not reported in the newspapers had done much to condition the thinking of naval leaders.

On May 31, 1936, a party of enlisted men and one lieutenant from the USS *Blackhawk* were sightseeing in Chinwangtao, in northern China. One of them took pictures of a train carrying Japanese military equipment and was then forcibly detained by Japanese army officers who demanded his camera. This he refused to give up, although in their presence he did remove and destroy the film. The U.S.

officer subsequently informed the Japanese officers that he considered their actions totally unwarranted; that any difficulties with American sailors should be first referred to him; and that "above all they just keep their hands off American sailors." One of the Japanese officers said, "Sorry, I didn't know you were in town."[3]

Nearly two months later, in Peiping the American Ambassador, Mr. Nelson Trusler Johnson, learned of the incident. At that time he met with Admiral Orin Gould Murfin, Commander in Chief, Asiatic Fleet. They agreed that it was too late to take any action but that future instances should be promptly reported to the embassy or to the nearest consular office. Commanding officers, Navy and Marine, would have many opportunities in the next few years to do just that.

One of the most frustrating problems facing U.S. naval war planners was the almost complete lack of intelligence on the Japanese activities in the mandated islands. The presence of military bases, even small ones capable of supporting submarines or aircraft, posed a threat to any ship steaming toward Guam or the Philippines. In fact, Guam was effectively surrounded by Japanese controlled potential island bases. Japan had been given a mandate in 1919 under the provisions of Article 22 of the Covenant of the League of Nations to administer all former German islands north of the equator, but the same article also forbade the construction of fortifications. Since Japan had left the League of Nations in 1933 rather than accept a censure over her invasion of Manchuria, there was a strong possibility that the mandate against fortifications might not be honored. Early U.S. war plans had called for immediate reinforcement of the Philippines in the event of war; later plans were more realistic, calling for a progressive movement across the Pacific and seizure of islands as necessary. Under either contingency, effective planning depended on knowledge of enemy capabilities in the islands that stretched along the shortest route to Japan.

On occasion the Navy relieved ships in the Asiatic Fleet with others from "stateside," and such ships, en route to the Asiatic stations, passed near the islands. To get close enough to observe bases and defense works necessitated entering Japanese territorial waters, and that required prior permission. An opportunity to see first-hand what was going on presented itself neatly when the USS *Alden* was scheduled to report to the Asiatic Fleet.

In a letter of June 5, 1936, Secretary of the Navy Claude Swanson presented his case to Secretary of State Cordell Hull, through whose department the request for visit clearance would have to go. He pointed out that for some time there had been "a strong undercurrent of conjecture and suspicion regarding the harbor development or fortification of the Pacific possessions of both the United States and Japan." To allay any such suspicion which might be held by the Japanese government, the Navy Department "would welcome the visits this year by two Japanese public vessels to certain of the Aleutian Islands and other ports not normally open to foreign vessels." And then followed the gambit—would the State Department inform the Japanese government regarding the proposed trip of this destroyer and suggest the desirability of an invitation from that government for the *Alden* "to visit informally certain of the larger unopened ports of the Mandated Islands, as well as the open ports of Saipan, Anguar, Palau, Ponape, Jaluit, and Truk?"[4]

The American ambassador to Japan, Joseph Grew, was so advised. His answer a few days later was not optimistic. He had made an informal suggestion that an invitation be extended to the *Alden* to visit the closed ports of the Japanese mandated islands. However, he observed that "it is quite possible that the Minister of Foreign Affairs will avoid communicating to me the unfavorable reply and will tacitly let the matter drop." If the foreign minister chose the face-saving approach of just not extending the invitation, Grew could see that nothing would be gained by pressing for an answer. He informed Hull that if a definite answer was desired—even though it might be negative—he would seek another interview with the foreign minister a few days before July 21,[5] the date the *Alden* was scheduled to depart Hawaii. The Navy desired an answer if possible before that date.

On July 13, Captain Bruce Livingston Canaga and Captain William Dilworth Puleston of the Central Division of the office of the Chief of Naval Operations inquired of Mr. Max Hamilton of the Far Eastern Division of the State Department if anything further had been heard from Tokyo in regard to the visit of the *Alden* to the closed ports. Hamilton informed the captains that the approach, in this instance, reaction was that if the Japanese did not respond favorably to the approach which had been made by Mr. Grew, then the American government should notify the Japanese government in the usual way that the *Alden* desired to visit the *open* ports of the mandated islands. Mr. Hamilton informed the captains that the approach, in this instance, had been based at least partially upon the thought that the Japanese might wish to extend such an invitation as a good will gesture, and that it would be better to await the outcome of the present approach before requesting visits to the open ports. Both Canaga and Puleston indicated they concurred with Hamilton but that they would discuss the matter with the Chief of Naval Operations, Admiral William Harrison Standley, to see if he wanted Grew to press the foreign minister for a definite answer.[6]

The next day Admiral Standley conferred with his staff from the War Plans and Central Divisions on the subject of the *Alden* visit in the light of Grew's telegram. The following morning, July 15, Commander Harry Wilbur Hill of the central division, on orders of Admiral Standley, called Hamilton to say that Admiral Standley *did* want Mr. Grew to press the Japanese foreign minister for a "definitive reply." The reason given for this hard stand by the Navy was that "in the past we had never been able to get a formal reply from the Japanese Government [granting] permission for American naval vessels to visit *closed* ports in the Japanese Mandated Islands." If the Japanese opposed visiting *closed* ports Mr. Grew was to "notify the Japanese Government that the Navy Department desired to have the U.S.S. *Alden* visit certain *open* ports" and, failing to get this concession, the "Government might have on record any disposition on the part of the Japanese Government to raise objection to visits of American naval vessels to *open* ports of the Mandated Islands."[7]

A formal request at this juncture for the *Alden* to visit the *open* ports would have put Ambassador Grew in an undesirable position. Having entered into informal discussion in a spirit of good will and asking for a mutual exchange of visits to show good faith, he was being asked by the Navy Department to change his approach to a more demanding, formal one in which a definite answer would be required instead of the more discrete diplomatic silence. If the foreign minister, for reasons which he could not disclose, could not give an affirmative answer, he still was in a position to keep friendly relations by remaining silent. To force the issue after having tried to get mutual visits by the informal gambit would most probably embarrass the foreign minister and strain the existing good relations. In addition, requesting to visit the open ports without waiting for an answer to the informal request to visit all ports would make it particularly difficult for the Japanese to accept, for it would show the actual motive was to see the mandated islands and not to promote good will by mutual visits.

On July 16, the U.S. Navy gave up its insistence on forcing a Japanese decision. Admiral Standley, "after some consideration . . . thought the best thing to do would be to let the case of the . . . *Alden* run its course; to send no further instructions on this case to Mr. Grew;" and should the *Alden* not receive an invitation to visit to proceed to the Asiatic station. Mr. Hamilton was informed that another attempt would be made after the first of the year when a transport was scheduled to go to the Far East. Then the request would be made to visit open ports through the regular diplomatic channels.[8] For the time being, the naval planners would have neither the benefit of a visit nor the satisfaction of being told "no" for the record.

If the naval officers were frustrated over not being able to force the Japanese through diplomatic channels to allow U.S. naval vessels to visit the mandated islands, their frustrations were to increase to the multiple power over not getting State Department cooperation in closing Hawaiian ports to Japanese visits. For years visits by Japanese naval vessels to the Hawaiian ports of Hilo, and Honolulu, were a cause for much alarm among the intelligence and security officers in the Hawaiian commands. The largest foreign ethnic group in the islands was Japanese and such visits were usually festive with deliberate programs to promote goodwill on the part of the Japanese Navy and the local Japanese citizens. Numerous instances of photographing of facilities, measuring piers and buildings, and exchange of packages were observed by American personnel. In Hilo, lack of customs and immigration officials made the problems of control even worse.

In June 1936, a joint planning committee met in Honolulu to study ways to take action against suspected espionage in the Hawaiian chain. Representatives from the Departments of War, Commerce, Treasury, State, and Navy attended. The Chief of Naval Operations forwarded information of Japanese activities as discussed in Honolulu to the President.

On August 10, 1936, in a memorandum to the Chief of Naval Operations the President expressed himself in very positive language:

> One obvious thought occurs to me—that every Japanese citizen or non-citizen on the Island of Oahu who meets these Japanese ships or has any connection with their officers or men should be secretly but definitely identified and his or her name placed on a special list of those who would be the first to be placed in a concentration camp in the event of trouble.
>
> As I told you verbally today, I think a Joint Board should consider and adopt plans relating to the Japanese population of all the Islands. Decision should be made as to whether the Island of Hawaii could or should be defended against landing parties. From my personal observation I should say off-hand that it would be extraordinarily difficult, as the Island is quite far from Oahu. The chief objective should be to prevent its occupation as a base of operations against Oahu and other islands.[9]

This was the Commander in Chief of all U.S. armed forces speaking about concentration camps for citizens as well as aliens. They would be used, not in 1936 but in 1942, and not in Hawaii but in California. The Japanese threat to Oahu would come not from a base of operations on Hawaii, but from fast and efficient aircraft carriers. Ironically, Oahu would be hit first.

If Roosevelt felt concern over Japanese actions in the Hawaiian Islands, he was equally concerned about the other large group of American islands much closer to Japan's expanding sphere of influence. The Philippine Islands had been guaranteed their independence prior to 1946 by the Tydings-McDuffie Act of 1934. Army planners considered the islands indefensible, whereas Navy planners wanted to build up naval facilities both in the Philippines and in Guam. The expiration of the naval limitations agreements made such possibilities "legal" again.

On November 16, 1936, shortly after his re-election, the President discussed the future of the Philippines relative to Japan with Robert Walton Moore, acting secretary of state, and Francis Bowes Sayre, assistant secretary of state, who was later to become United States high commissioner to the Philippines. The diplomats asked Roosevelt whether he had reached a decision with respect to the retention of a naval base in the Philippines after the granting of independence. Specifically they raised the question of the defensibility of such a naval base, pointing out that an indefensible base "would clearly constitute a liability rather than an asset." Roosevelt's answer was prophetic; "that in case of a Japanese attack upon the Philippines we would have to let the Philippines go temporarily and that we would gradually be moving westward, making our position secure on one Pacific island after another as we slowly moved West."[10] He estimated that it would take at least two years after hostilities commenced before the U.S. would be prepared for an open attack upon the Japanese forces.

Sayre, still not satisfied, suggested that the whole question of Philippine neutralization and our future program there turned on "whether a Philippine naval base is defensible." Roosevelt said that he was not convinced either way and that he would have the War and Navy Departments prepare a memorandum on this question. He added that the War Department would undoubtedly feel such a naval base to be indefensible except by acquiring and making secure an extended area around it. "The Navy, on the other hand, might feel it possible to defend an isolated point such as Gibraltar."[11] Disagreement over defense arrangements would persist until Japanese victories traumatically ended that interservice debate.

7

While Roosevelt discussed the future of the Philippines with State Department representatives in Washington, Admiral Harry Ervin Yarnell, who had just assumed duty as Commander in Chief, Asiatic Fleet, made his first report to the Chief of Naval Operations. He wrote that "the subject that the British intelligence officers and others seemed more concerned with than any other in their conversations with our officers related to the future status of the Philippines." The British were incredulous that the United States would leave the "Philippines to its political fate and withdraw all United States protection from the gateway to Singapore and India." Senior British officers thought that the Japanese menace could only be met with British-American cooperation and that the Japanese "southward expansion policy" could be prevented by a strong naval base in the Philippines plus the Singapore base.[12]

Cooperation with the British as well as the French and Dutch became a consistent theme for Yarnell, as did his request for a tougher United States policy in the Far East. The issue of Singapore, how it would be used and by whom, along with the problems inherent in the defense of the Philippines, would be constantly in the conversations between the United States and Britain for the next five years. Long after Yarnell had left the Asiatic Station, cooperative defense plans for Singapore and the Philippines would still be in the discussion phase. A meeting in Manila, December 4–6, 1941, between General Douglas MacArthur, Admiral Thomas Charles Hart, successor to Yarnell as Commander in Chief, Asiatic Fleet, and British Admiral Tom Phillips was an eleventh-hour attempt to reach agreement on matters which concerned Yarnell and his British contemporaries in 1936.

CHAPTER 2

Japan Commences Aggression in China

The answer to President Roosevelt's question concerning war plans originated in the War Plans Division of the Office of the Chief of Naval Operations. In addition to being an important part of the CNO staff, that division was also part of the Joint Board and Joint Planning Committee.

The Joint Board, which decided probable enemies, was the oldest of the interservice agencies, established in July 1903, by agreement between the service secretaries without statutory authorization. The need had always existed to coordinate planning between the two services, but the Spanish-American War with its overseas operations and logistic problems brought the urgency of joint planning to the forefront. The board was suspended, strangely enough, in 1913 and 1914 by President Woodrow Wilson because "he did not wish it to enter discussions of subjects that he considered to be the President's preogative and that might lead to political repercussions." The board "renewed its meetings in October 1915, and was finally reconsituted by new orders at the end of World War I."[1] The new charter for the Joint Board specified the membership to be the Army Chief of Staff and his deputy chief of staff and assistant chief of staff for war plans, the Chief of Naval Operations, the assistant chief of naval operations, and the director of the war plans division.

The Joint Board was consultative and advisory to the Commander in Chief and took no executive action unless required to do so by higher authority. There were no required meetings of the Joint Board, en masse, unless there were matters to be discussed. The organization which permitted the Chief of Staff, the Chief of Naval Operations, and their immediate assistants not to waste time in unnecessary meetings was the working arm of the Joint Board, the Joint Planning Committee. Made up of the War Plans Division chiefs and their assistants, the committee met often, discussed their particular problems with other services' representatives, reached an understanding, and presented the tentative agreement to the Joint Board. Usually there was no discussion in the Joint Board meetings on tentative agreements, since both service chiefs kept informed on subjects by briefing and being briefed by their war plans officers. Discussions in the Joint Planning Committee conferences in reality reflected the views of the Chief of Staff and the Chief of Naval Operations. Disagreements which could not be resolved during Joint Board meetings were to be decided by the President, if necessary. The biggest area of dispute between the Army and Navy in 1936 and 1937 was over war plans in the Pacific—whether to plan on taking the offensive in case of war with Japan (Navy's position) or hold a defense line through Alaska-Hawaii-Panama (Army's position). Chief of Staff of the Army General Malin Craig, evidently shared the views of his planners, but he was either unable or unwilling to have the dispute brought before the President for decision.[2]

In the immediate aftermath of World War I, the Joint Board, in an idealistic general staff approach, undertook to prepare detailed plans for action in any conceivable emergency. A color was assigned as the code word for each emergency and applied as well to the country visualized as the enemy in that emergency. *Orange* was the code word for Japan and actions against Japan while *Red* applied to the British Empire. *Blue* for the United States was less a war plan than a plan for the national position of the American military forces in certain contingencies with no particular enemy specified. Most of the hypothetical situations were highly improbable in the peacetime era of the 1920s. The major exception was the *Orange Plan,* for war against Japan. That plan, from its inception, called for moving large Army units to the Philippines and extensive naval operations in the western Pacific.

Partially as a result of the naval staff review of the *Orange Plan* for Captain Bastedo's use in answering the President and partially because of the increased affinity of Japan for Nazi Germany, the Joint Board, on March 17, 1937, restudied the existing *Orange Plan.* There was an obvious need for a reappraisal of the ability of the Navy to protect troop movements to the Philippines and to carry a war to the western Pacific and, even more, the ever-diminishing ability of the Army to muster any level of expeditionary forces to go anywhere. "By successive stages the strength of the Army was cut and cut until in 1935 it had declined to 118,750,"[3] and yet from its initial appearance in 1924 to its cancellation in 1938 the *Orange Plan* called for the Army within ten days of the start of hostilities to have 50,000 troops on the West Coast ready to sail to the Philippines. After months of wrestling with unknown capabilities and known deficiencies the Joint Board agreed on November 16, 1937 to rescind the existing *Orange Plan* and to prepare a substitute. The war planners had tasted another bitter dose of revising plans downward to match existing and fore-seeable capabilities against an increasingly stronger enemy whose intentions were changing for the worse.

While the War Plans Division officers grappled with the shortcomings of the *Orange Plan,* the officers in the Central Division continued to maneuver through diplomatic channels for permission to visit the mandated islands. After the Japanese declination of Ambassador Grew's informal bid to get the *Alden* into the islands as part of a mutual visit exchange, the Navy Department decided to try the formal route of request with the next westbound ship. That proved to be the transport *Gold Star.*

In February 1937, the Navy Department requested through the State Department permission for the *Gold Star* to make informal visits at Saipan, Yokohama, Kobe, Miike, Palau, and Truk. After months of waiting for a reply, the American ambassador finally received the inevitable decision. Answering a telegram from the State Department, sent at the request of the Navy Department, "inquiring whether the proposed informal visits of the USS *Gold Star* to certain ports in the Japanese Mandated Islands would be agreeable to the Japanese Government," Mr. Grew stated that he was "in receipt of a reply from the Foreign Office . . . dated July 31, 1937, stating that the Japanese Government is unable to give consent to the proposed visit."[4] No reason was given since none was required, but the fact that earlier in the month Japan had renewed the conflict with China indicated an unwillingness to be involved with American visits at that time. No follow-up requests for other visits appear in the archive files; evidently the Navy gave up trying to get Japanese permission to visit even the open ports in the mandated islands.

In the Japanese home islands the story was different. There United States naval ships visited frequently and generally were well received. Usually during a tour in the China Station, the Commander in Chief, Asiatic Fleet, made a formal visit to Japan. As Admiral Yarnell had not visited Japan since taking command of the Asiatic Fleet, he planned to visit that country in the summer of 1937. In May he also requested authorization from the State Department through Navy Department channels to visit Vladivostok in July. Since the visits of an admiral of a fleet had political ramifications in the diplomatic sense, especially if a second country was involved in the visit, the State Department advised the ambassador in Tokyo of Yarnell's tentative plans. The State Department message also stated that it might possibly be advantageous from the point of view of "psychological effects, both positive and negative, upon Soviet and Japanese officialdom, for Yarnell to make the visits to Vladivostok and to Japan on and as part of one trip rather than as separate and therefore more conspicuously special visits."[5] Mr. Grew was directed to discuss the matter with his naval attache and then to pass the suggestion for a combined visit to Admiral Yarnell for his consideration.

The ambassador replied the following week that the naval attache concurred in his opinion that a naval visit to Japan during the summer months should be avoided, and that he had recommended to Admiral Yarnell that he consider a visit between October 1 and October 20 or after November 15 due to Japanese naval and military maneuvers between those dates. If those dates were not convenient a spring visit was suggested. The naval attache further advised Admiral Yarnell, with Mr. Grew's concurrence, that the same political ends would be gained if the announcements of the proposed visits to Vladivostok and to Japan be concurrent but that the visits themselves need not be concurrent.[6]

The recommendation that the summer months should be avoided was very prophetic. On July 7, 1937, the Japanese invaded China following an incident near Marco Polo Bridge, which spanned the Yunting River just south of Peiping and on the strategic Peiping-Hankow railway. Admiral Yarnell had to forego his formal visits for more active relations with the Japanese in China.

Fleet exercises had kept Admiral Yarnell from visiting Japanese ports in the late spring of 1937. By coincidence the same situation in reverse gave the U.S. Navy an excuse to deny visits by Japanese ships to San Francisco. Visits by four naval transports to West Coast ports had been proposed by the Japanese for May and June. Since the United States Fleet was scheduled to arrive in San Francisco May 28 and depart June 4, the Navy Department had the pleasure of telling the State Department to inform the Japanese "that they neither arrive at nor depart from San Francisco on the two dates mentioned."[7]

The year before the Marco Polo Bridge incident ushered in the last phase of the Sino-Japanese War a third and final revision had been made in Japanese national defense policy. The Japanese counterpart to the American *Orange Plan* was in actuality two plans, one by the Navy portraying the United States as the enemy and one by the Army which focused on the Soviet Union. After years of competition with the Army, the Navy had won its case with an imperial ruling approving its rationale for building up strength for a southward expansion. The Army would build up its strength to counter the Soviet Union and to secure the empire's position on the continent and, concomitantly, the Navy would advance Japanese military and economic interests to the south. The threat of British, American, and Dutch opposition and even the possibility of a clash of arms were recognized. To meet such opposition the naval budget in 1936 was sharply increased to provide for an additional two battleships, two aircraft carriers, fifteen destroyers and thirteen submarines. Having formally denounced the naval treaties with Britain and the United States, the Japanese Navy obviously was entering into a buildup of capital ship forces for supremacy in the western Pacific. Control of the western Pacific against the United States Fleet was considered possible only with a force of twelve battleships and twelve aircraft carriers. The ships funded with the increase in 1936 provided the final increment for the force goals.

The inauguration of the war in 1937 in northern China was planned and executed by the Japanese Army. The objective was to annex more territory for expansion—hopefully at as cheap a price as the Army had paid for Manchuria—and to gain a strategic advantage over the Soviet Union and China, while Premier Joseph Stalin ruthlessly purged his general officers and before Generalissimo Chiang Kai-shek became any stronger. It was not the intent of the Army at the time to engage in a general offensive against China. However, agreement had been reached in 1936 between the general staffs of the Army and Navy that the Army would protect Japanese nationals and interests in Shanghai if needed and would deploy three divisions to central China if relations with China were further strained. After action started in northern China the Navy lost no time in invoking the Army promise for help in Shanghai and central China. The southern expansion plan was under way.

The Navy plan urged upon the general staffs by Vice Admiral Kiyoshi Hasegawa, commander of the Japanese Third Fleet in Shanghai, involved immediate occupation of Shanghai and Nanking and the destruction of the Chinese air force. This, reasoned the Navy, would force China to surrender. More was at stake than a quick victory over China. Shanghai, with its International Settlement, was the economic nerve center of the Far East. France, Italy, Japan, the United States and, especially, Britain had sizable investments in Shanghai and the Yangtze valley which they managed from their respective sectors in the International Settlement. A Japanese-controlled Shanghai and a subservient China would give Japan definite economic advantages over its western rivals.

The 40,000 foreign residents of the International Settlement were self-governed by an elected council, although each of the foreign powers considered its own sector to be part of its national territory. *In toto* there existed a system of extraterritorial rights uniquely and inextricably woven, with each power protecting its sector with a small military force. Just as the American sector was patrolled by American Marines, the Japanese sector was protected by a naval landing party of 2,000. In July this force was reinforced by 300 sailors from Japanese ships in Shanghai and by an additional 1,000 from a squadron of fifteen ships which arrived on August 11. An incident over the shooting of a Japanese lieutenant and seaman, supposedly by the Chinese, provided the *cause célèbre* for pouring troops into Shanghai. The mayor of Shanghai, O. K. Yui, protested the increase in Japanese forces while the Japanese consul general, Suemasa Okamoto, objected to Chinese troop movements near the Japanese sector. Civilian control on both sides rapidly gave way to military control and operations. Unexpected Chinese resistance accelerated the influx of troops into the Shanghai area. On August 15, the Japanese government decided to send troops to Shanghai, in what appeared to be more than just a rerun of a similar plot in 1932.

At this time Admiral Yarnell, aboard the flagship *Augusta* in Shanghai, asked for "about 1000 Marines from the United States, as soon as practicable."[8] The United States then had in China 528 U.S. Marines at Peiping, 786 Army troops at Tientsin in accordance with the Boxer Protocol of 1901, and the Fourth Marine Regiment of 1,073 men in Shanghai. The Marines had been in Shanghai since 1927; they had been augmented by an army regiment during the 1932 disorders. The Asiatic Fleet under Yarnell's control was more a collection of ships to show the flag in the Far East than a balanced or even operational fleet. It consisted of one cruiser, approximately twelve destroyers, six submarines and six specially-built shallow draft river gunboats and auxiliaries. Only the gunboats remained exclusively in Chinese waters. The only modern ship in the entire fleet was the heavy cruiser *Augusta*. The fleet usually spent winter months in the Philippines and the summer months in Chefoo and Tsingtao in northern China.

The President agreed to a proposal to send the Sixth Marine Regiment from San Diego to Shanghai in answer to Admiral Yarnell's request. The decision was due in no small measure to the reasoned memoranda of Dr. Stanley K. Hornbeck, adviser on political relations in the State Department, and the fact that the British and French were reinforcing their garrisons also.[9]

While Admiral Yarnell had a box seat for the sparring around Shanghai, he became directly involved in the Japanese attempts to muscle into the area. An order from Vice Admiral Hasegawa closing part of the Yangtze to all shipping during hours of darkness without prior notification was sent through the Japanese and American consuls general. Admiral Yarnell shot back an indignant reply via the reverse of the route through which he had learned of Hasegawa's oral order. He took Hasegawa to task for not having conferred with him on the matter and then informed him that he was unable to comply because he must have freedom of action to move on short notice to visit men-of-war, merchantmen and U.S. Marines and bluejackets in the American sector. However, in order to facilitate identification in darkness he would arrange for each American ship to burn "navigation lights and fly her ensign or national flag as the case may be and to pass as close as practicable to the first Japanese man-of-war encountered up or down stream, reducing speed while passing her."[10] Yarnell's reply, which was paralleled by similar replies from the British and French naval commanders in chief, had several effects. For one, Admiral Hasegawa began to correspond directly with the other senior naval officers. One week later, on August 26, when Hasegawa proclaimed via the press that the lower Yangtze and coast of central China would be closed to Chinese shipping, he made a point to specify that his action "does not affect foreign . . . shipping."[11]

The third and most positive reaction to Yarnell's reply to Hasegawa was from Mr. Hull. On August 10, Mr. Hull had sent to Ambassador Johnson the State ". . . Department's concept of the mission and function of the United States armed forces in China." The key words in a rather long telegram were:

> . . . The primary function of these forces is to provide special protection for American nationals. Incidental to protection of life comes protection of property, but protection of property as such is not a primary objective. These forces are in no sense expeditionary forces. . . . nor are

15

they defending territory of the United States. They are expected to protect lives but they are not expected to hold positions regardless of hazards.[12]

At the end of Hull's message he directed Ambassador Johnson to

...repeat this telegram to Peiping, Tientsin, Shanghai, and Tsingtao, and instruct the officers in charge at those places to bring the contents of this telegram informally and in confidence to the attention of the commanding officers of American armed forces at those places.[13]

In view of the telegram of August 10, Mr. Hull was quite perturbed to receive directly from Admiral Yarnell nine days later the gist of Admiral Hasegawa's oral order and Yarnell's reply thereto. Within hours of the receipt of Yarnell's telegram Mr. Hull had sent to Mr. Clarence Edward Gauss, the consul general Shanghai, the first in a series of what were to become increasingly acrimonious messages meant for Admiral Yarnell. Hull referred to the August 10 telegram and said that he assumed "that the contents of that telegram were brought to the attention of the commanding officers of American armed forces." It was the desire of the government to protect its nationals, but also to avoid becoming in any way involved in the conflict between the Chinese and Japanese or to interfere with their military operations. More specifically, Mr. Hull assumed that "our armed forces will to as great an extent as possible avoid coming into or remaining in line of fire between Japanese and Chinese armed forces and, if in such line of fire, will not make assumption that fire is being deliberately directed against them unless such is with reasonable clearness the case." Then followed: "This is not an instruction or an order; it represents an effort to be of assistance... Please bring the above to the attention of the Commander-in-Chief at once."[14]

On September 1, Admiral Yarnell reported to the Chief of Naval Operations, Admiral William Daniel Leahy, progress on preparations to deny entrance of armed Chinese and Japanese troops into the American sector of the International Settlement. The Marines had barbed wire and multiple machine guns along the front facing the Japanese sector. The anticipated "enemy" can be surmised by the last sentence in the message: "Unarmed Chinese soldiers will be permitted to enter and will be segregated under guard."[15]

On September 2, the Japanese announced a tightening of the blockade of the Yangtze and requested notification of the intended entry and exit of American commercial vessels. Mr. Hull's instruction to the consul general at Shanghai, meant directly for Admiral Yarnell, was that there need be no objection "to the giving of such notifications, but that if and as notifications are given they should be given on the basis of courtesy and practical expediency rather than on the basis of a waiving of the right to immunity from interference which the giving of an express promise on our part would imply."[16] Admiral Yarnell was told that he should neither refuse nor agree to comply but should state that notification would be given to both Chinese and Japanese when and so far as practicable. Yarnell chafed under these instructions for the next three weeks. The vagueness of orders, a subsequent prohibition against giving general directions to American shipping in China, and disagreement over actions relative to the Japanese prompted Yarnell to issue his own policy statement. On September 22, he sent a copy to the Chief of Naval Operations, after having issued it to officers in the Asiatic Fleet and releasing it to the press in China. Admiral Leahy conferred with Dr. Hornbeck in the State Department and decided to release Yarnell's policy statement to the press in Washington since it had already been given to the press in Shanghai. Immediately afterward President Roosevelt sent a memorandum to Secretary of State Hull saying that he was "disturbed by the newspaper story a few days ago..." He could not "understand why this statement by Admiral Yarnell, relating to American policy in China, should have been handled by the Navy press room, nor [did he] know whether its release had [Hull's] approval beforehand or not."[17] The feelings of the President and Mr. Hull were made known to Admiral Leahy, who promptly told Admiral Yarnell that it was "desired that hereafter any statement regarding 'policy' contemplated by the Commander-in-Chief Asiatic Fleet be referred to the Secretary of the Navy for approval."[18]

Admiral Yarnell's policy statement which caused so much furor read in part:

> The policy of Cincaf during the present emergency is to employ United States naval forces under his command so as to offer all possible protection and assistance to our nationals in cases where needed... Most American citizens now in China are engaged in businesses or professions...these persons are unwilling to leave until their businesses have been destroyed or they are forced to leave due to actual physical danger. Until such time comes our naval forces can not be withdrawn without failure in our duty and without bringing discredit on the United States Navy. In giving assistance and protection our naval forces may at times be exposed to dangers which will in cases be slight but in any case these risks must be accepted.[19]

Though the statement might have been bothersome to President Roosevelt and Mr. Hull, it was in actuality quite an accurate blueprint for policy followed by Yarnell and his successor, Admiral Hart.

While the Japanese forces advanced up the Yangtze River in the fall of 1937, the Secretary of State received two letters which presaged a crisis involving the United States and Japan. On September 14, the Chief of Naval Operations reported that, except for occasional purchases in Netherlands Borneo and Oha in North Sakhalin, the Japanese imported all their oil from the United States.[20] Two weeks later the Secretary of the Navy passed to the State Department information on an order for 3,500,000 barrels of crude oil for the Japanese Navy to be shipped from the United States between November 1, 1937 and March 1, 1938. The contract called for an export rate of 875,000 barrels per month which was $2\frac{1}{2}$ times the rate of the preceding eighteen months. In addition to building up her capital ship inventory Japan had started in earnest to build up her oil reserves. For four years she would be allowed to draw upon American resources, much to the consternation of those in and out of government who wanted to restrict her imports from the United States.

By September the Japanese were in position to hit Nanking with the full strength of their naval air force. Admiral Hasegawa gave notice that bombing would begin after twelve o'clock noon on September 21. Upon receipt of this information Admiral Yarnell sent his Japanese counterpart a letter telling him that the United States Navy had at Nanking two gun boats, the *Luzon* and *Guam* and that "as long as the United States Embassy and U.S. nationals remain in Nanking, it [was] necessary for these two vessels to remain there also." These two vessels had a large United States flag spread horizontally on "the upper works." Yarnell requested that the Japanese naval air force be given instructions "to avoid dropping bombs in the vicinity of these vessels."[21] Through September, October, and November the gun boats enjoyed immunity from bomb damage.

The month of October 1937 emphasized the tenor of the time. A frustrated President Roosevelt made a speech on October 5, in which he stated that international lawlessness and war, declared or undeclared, should be treated as contagious and quarantined. His implication was that the United States was considering action to assist other nations in the quarantine. Pressure from Mr. Hull, reaction from the many isolationist congressmen, and disapproval by most of the press forced a recantation of the initiation of international restraints just one week later. Hard on the heels of Roosevelt's about-face, Admiral

Yarnell sent the Secretary of State a message that caused more than just a ripple in the sea that Mr. Hull had lately helped calm down. Admiral Yarnell's message was a copy of instructions given to the Commanding General, U.S. Marines, at Shanghai:

> In case of attack on the defense forces or noncombatants in the United States sector by planes of any nationality fire may be opened on such planes in self defense.[22]

Admiral Yarnell pointed out to the Secretary of State that his order was just an extension of one already given to vessels of the Asiatic Fleet authorizing them to take such action in case of attack. In a concurrent message to Admiral Leahy, Yarnell stated that he believed such attacks were improbable but "issuance and publicity of this order will undoubtedly result in more care being observed in avoiding such action by planes of opposing forces."[23]

The day after receiving the Yarnell order, Max Hamilton of the Far Eastern Division on orders from Mr. Hull called on Admiral Richardson, the assistant chief of naval operations, not "to raise the question as to the merits of the order issued by Admiral Yarnell" but to point out "that the Secretary of State felt that the giving of publicity to such an order [created] serious embarrassment to the Secretary of State in the moderate course which he was endeavoring to follow in foreign relations." Hamilton pointed out that "public sentiment and sensational newspaper reports in regards to such orders played into the hands of the critics of the Administration," and that in the past when Admiral Yarnell had issued certain orders with sensational publicity in the American press the President had spoken to the Secretary of State about the matter. Admiral Richardson was told "if Admiral Yarnell could not be directed to refrain from giving publicity to such matters, Mr. Hull would lay the whole matter before the President for decision."[24] Admiral Richardson discussed the question of muzzling Admiral Yarnell with Admiral Leahy who in turn informed the Secretary of the Navy. The decision was relayed back to the State Department that Admiral Yarnell had a great many troubles of his own and that the Navy did not wish to send him the instruction requested by Mr. Hull. The next morning, October 30, Mr. Sumner Welles, the under secretary of state, called the President and received concurrence that the Navy Department should send a telegram to Admiral Yarnell asking him to endeavor to avoid publicity in such matters. The President, as Commander in Chief had made his decision and the Commander in Chief, Asiatic Fleet, was so ordered.[25]

As the Japanese closed in on Nanking in the fall of 1937 Chiang Kai-shek's Foreign Office advised the American ambassador, Mr. Johnson, to evacuate. On November 22, the ambassador and most of the embassy staff departed on the *Luzon* up the Yangtze to Hankow, while the *Panay*, which had replaced the *Guam*, remained in Nanking to evacuate the remainder of the staff. Mr. Grew notified the Japanese government of the *Panay*'s planned movements on December 1, 1937. On December 12, the *Panay*, carrying embassy personnel and escorting three American-owned self-propelled oil barges, was bombed and strafed by Japanese aircraft despite the weather being clear and sunny and the large American flags at the masts and painted on the awnings. The attack sank the *Panay* and two oil barges, wounded eleven officers and men, and killed two sailors and a civilian.

On orders of Admiral Yarnell the United States held a court of inquiry in Shanghai into the facts of the sinking while the State Department, on orders from the President, demanded "an apology, indemnities, punishment of officers involved and assurances that similar incidents would not happen again." The findings of the court of inquiry were sent by the State Department to the Japanese government on December 23, on which date the Japanese accepted the four demands originally ordered by Roosevelt. Indemnities of $2,214,000 were paid by the Japanese on request of the State Department after agreement with the Navy Department on valuation of the various items in the claims.

In the latter part of November Admiral Yarnell had suggested withdrawing the Sixth Marines. Fighting had progressed up the Yangtze and the British had indicated that they were reducing the size of their force. The State Department agreed but requested that a formal announcement not be made until the transport was actually in China in the event that something might occur and that the Navy Department get in touch before giving the press release "to safeguard against any statement which would imply that the Marines had been sent to Shanghai for 'fighting purposes.' "[26] On December 10, a press release from Shanghai carried the story that the Sixth Marines from San Diego would return on the *Chaumont* in January. Since Yarnell had asked for the Marines in the first place, the State Department acquiesced in his decision to send them home.

On December 21, the Commander in Chief of the Japanese fleet in China issued a letter to the European and American naval commanders that "it is the desire of the Japanese Navy that foreign vessels including warships will refrain from navigating the Yangtze except when clear understanding is reached with us."[27] The joint letter from the American, French, British, and Italian commanders said in reply that with regards to the movements of warships, they would of course notify the Japanese authorities on the river of intended movement whenever practicable, but that they could not accept the restriction suggested by the Japanese letter that foreign men-of-war could not move freely without prior arrangement with the Japanese and that they reserved the right to move their ships whenever necessary without notification.[28]

Four days after Admiral Yarnell had reported the exchange with the Commander in Chief, Japanese Fleet in China, the Secretary of the Navy informed him that his "continued presence . . . in Shanghai [was] thought to be desirable from the political and diplomatic point of view." Admiral Yarnell was to remain in Shanghai until March 1938 when, by order of the President, he was released from the geographical restrictions on his movements.

As 1937 drew to a close, Secretary of State Hull could take some satisfaction in having avoided a direct confrontation with the Japanese despite Admiral Yarnell's propensity for taking positive stands against each of the Japanese restrictions. Hull assiduously parried each suggestion by the British that—jointly with the United States—economic sanctions be taken against the Japanese and, even more horrifying to Hull, that jointly a naval show of strength be made in the Far East. In the United States the tide of isolationism was running strong and Hull correctly read the signs of the time. A case in point was the sinking of the *Panay*. Unlike the sinking of the *Maine* in Havana, Cuba, in 1898, which triggered a war cry, the attack on the *Panay* precipitated a hue and cry to get the United States military out of China. In fact, a Gallup poll one month after the sinking showed 70 percent of the American people in favor of *all* Americans, including missionaries, leaving China.

There was no satisfaction or comfort in the ranks of the military planners in December. As the joint planners struggled with the *Orange Plan* in the light of Japanese successes and impudence, it was readily apparent how weak the United States was. The only military strength available was the Navy—a one-ocean navy. Parsimonious congresses had appropriated such meager funds for the Army that after pay, which was fixed by statute, and repair and maintenance costs for the surplus World War I equipment, little was left to improve the weap-

21

ons inventory. The Navy had fared slightly better since President Roosevelt had taken the initiative to build it up to treaty strength, but the Congress did not authorize any increase in personnel strengths.

Admiral Leahy and his staff, aware of British interests and responsibilities in parts of the western Pacific and the possibility of future cooperation against a militant Japan, decided to conduct private conversations with the Admiralty. Actually, the conversations were to have a twofold purpose: to find out what could be done if the United States and Britain found themselves at war with Japan and to take up with the British the question of limitations on battleship displacement which had been stipulated in the London Treaty of 1935 and 1936. President Roosevelt agreed with the approach and the purpose of the visit. Leahy, with this approval, decided in late December, 1937, to send Captain Royal Eason Ingersoll, then chief of the War Plans Division, to converse with war planners in the Admiralty. His preparation was indicative of the significance of his trip, for in addition to being briefed by Admiral Leahy, he was also called to the White House for a briefing. His visit would set a precedent for similar meetings between representatives of the two navies which would in future years draw them together, not against Japan or in the Pacific, but against an enemy elsewhere. Interestingly, four years later, Ingersoll in the rank of admiral assumed duty as Commander in Chief, Atlantic Fleet, when British-American cooperation was the closest.

CHAPTER 3

American War Plans
Against Japan

Upon his arrival in London, Captain Ingersoll met with the British Secretary of State for Foreign Affairs, Sir Anthony Eden, who had cancelled a post-Christmas holiday for the occasion. Ingersoll told Eden that the United States Navy's plans for action in the Pacific were based on certain assumptions about the fleet dispositions the British might be able to make and that the same was probably true about British plans. President Roosevelt and Admiral Leahy thought the time had come "to carry matters a stage further by exchanging information in order to co-ordinate our plans more closely." Ingersoll was free to disclose the American dispositions under certain eventualities and desired to learn what the British dispositions would be under similar circumstances. In answer to Secretary Eden's question on possible courses of action then or in the future, Ingersoll replied that the discussions which were to be held between himself and the Admiralty "would be limited to future incidents against which joint action might later be taken, [but that] no move could be made at all in the Pacific, unless full preparation had been made for every eventuality, including war." Ingersoll thought the technical examination between the two countries should come first, after which any considerations on political decisions should be easier.[1] He left with the impression that Eden was more interested at the time in immediate gestures to impress the Japanese than he was in long-range planning. corresponding opposite in the War Plans Division of the Admiralty,

The technical talks were held between Captain Ingersoll and his Captain Tom Phillips. Ingersoll recorded his impressions during these talks in a daily report to the Chief of Naval Operations. As Ingersoll saw it, the British were not counting on any assistance from Russia,

France, or the Netherlands. They were interested in Manila as a base, because they feared Hong Kong was too vulnerable to land attack, and they were sure the Japanese would not attempt to take the Philippines while they were involved in China. They believed their positions in the Pacific would be safe with units of their fleet based at Singapore and the United States Fleet based at Hawaii or, better yet, to the westward of Hawaii. For an effective show of strength against the Japanese, the British proposed that their fleet start for Singapore and the United States Fleet for Hawaii to arrive approximately at the same time. Should the two governments decide to blockade Japan from further southward expansion, the two navies would hold a line roughly from Singapore through the Netherlands East Indies past New Guinea and the New Hebrides eastward of Australia and New Zealand. (This was the genesis of a plan of defense which would be debated, revised, and disputed until two days before the Pearl Harbor attack.) British officers believed that such a show of strength by the two navies might be necessary—even if there were no hostilities with Japan—in order to bring about peace terms between China and Japan which would have continued the principle of the "open door."[2]

Captains Ingersoll and Phillips signed the official "Record of Conversations" on January 12, 1938, and agreed therein to recommend British-U.S. cooperation in case of war with Japan, the British basing a fleet at Singapore and the United States concentrating a fleet at Pearl Harbor.[3]

While Captain Ingersoll was still in London, Admiral Yarnell in Shanghai was taking exception to the actions of Admiral Hasegawa. The first of the year Yarnell had learned through the British Navy of a new Japanese policy allowing only Japanese merchant ships to proceed up the Yangtze. He pointed out in a letter to Admiral Hasegawa on January 5 that, as recently as December 28, Ambassador Grew had informed the Japanese government "that the United States claimed absolute freedom for their ships to move and trade on the river and that the United States government looks to the Japanese authorities to give prior warning in regard to any area on the Yangtze becoming, through steps taken by them, a dangerous area." Then followed the strong language for which Admiral Yarnell would be criticized by Hull later: "I can not accept a policy which prevents the free navigation of the Yangtze River by United States naval or merchant vessels."[4] Yarnell's letter was ignored by the Japanese. They controlled the river above Nanking and in the name of military operations they also controlled ship movements on the river in that area for the rest of the year.

One week after Captain Ingersoll returned to Washington from London, his war planners—with their U.S. Army counterparts—rejected the latest version of the *Orange Plan* which had been prepared by the Joint Planning Committee. On January 19, the two service authorities on Pacific problems, Major General Stanley D. Embick and Rear Admiral James O. Richardson, were directed to make a further Pacific study. Embick, as a brigadier general, had designed the defenses of Corregidor and formerly commanded the harbor defenses of Manila and Subic Bays. In 1933 he wrote while in the Philippines, and later reiterated in 1935 while serving in the Army War Plans Division, that "to carry out the present *Orange Plan*—with the provisions for the early dispatch of our fleet to Philippine waters—would be literally an act of madness."[5] Richardson, who was then assistant chief of naval operations, was thoroughly familiar with the Navy's position and *Orange Plan* evolution. He also had first-hand experience in the Far East, having served two tours of duty with the Asiatic Fleet. The efforts of the pair were accepted as a new *Orange Plan* by the Joint Board on February 21 and by the service secretaries a week later.[6] On the basis of this latest plan, the Navy asked for and received from the President and Congress authorization for a 20 percent increase in size.

Concurrently, while the *Orange Plan* was being rewritten in Washington, Admiral Leahy wrote his two key fleet commanders to revise their supporting war plans. He told Admiral C. C. Bloch, Commander in Chief, United States Fleet, and Rear Admiral H. E. Yarnell, Commander in Chief, Asiatic Fleet, that in the event the United States and British governments should "at some indefinite time in the future" decide that parallel action be taken concerning policy in the Far East, certain assumptions would have to be made "in order to adopt existing *Orange* plans to changed situation"—in other words, "*Blue* and *Red* against *Orange*."[7]

Among the assumptions made by Admiral Leahy were three significant ones affecting future planning: (a) Should the British government decide to send a naval force to the Far East, it would send a force as a single tactical unit of sufficient strength "to engage the Japanese Fleet under normal tactical and strategical conditions" but in the event of a general war in Europe there would be a considerable reduction of British naval strength in the Far East. Under such conditions there would probably be required direct tactical cooperation between the United States and British fleets in the Pacific; (b) should the British government send its fleet to Singapore, the United States would send its fleet "to Truk or some other position in the same general area" after the decision is made "to dispatch the United States Fleet beyond the Hawaiian Islands;" and (c) should parallel action be decided upon by the two governments, "it can be assumed that the British will withdraw their garrisons in North China and the major units of the British China Fleet to Hong Kong or Singapore and that such withdrawals would probably be timed with the movement of the British Main Fleet to the Far East."[8] As events were to prove shortly, the assumptions that the British could station and maintain strong naval forces in Singapore or that the United States Fleet would or could move westward from Hawaii were short-lived dreams.

Through February and March 1938, a discussion brewed in the State Department over the advisability of the annual summer seasonal visit of Asiatic Fleet units to the northern China ports of Tsingtao and Chefoo. Both ports had been occupied rather peacefully by the Japanese since the visits of the year before. Max Hamilton, chief of the Far Eastern Division, in a memorandum to Secretary of State Hull on March 10, reasoned that although both cities were relatively free of disturbances—Chinese versus Japanese—there were possibilities of friction between Japanese troops and American sailors. The long campaign in China had tended "to affect adversely the morale and conduct of various units of the Japanese Army." The Japanese bombing of the *Panay* and other incidents involving the Japanese and American military units may also have tended "to ruffle the tempers of the rank and file of the American fleet."[9] The decision was made, however, for regular summer visits to Chefoo with occasional short visits from Chefoo to Tsingtao. The summer visit was to be shorter than in the past with fewer units participating. With the vantage point of hindsight one could have forecast the inevitable incidents.

While the degree of tension and likelihood of incidents increased in China between the Japanese and American military, the diplomats in Japan were writing the final chapter to the *Panay* tragedy. On April 22, Ambassador Grew received a check for $2,214,007.36 "as indemnification for losses to American property and for death and injuries of American citizens" incident to the *Panay* sinking. In presenting the check, the Japanese minister for foreign affairs raised some interesting points which truly rankled the officers in the Navy Department. Having paid indemnification, the Japanese government assumed it could, with propriety, salvage the sunken gunboat and two barges for conversion into scrap metal. After asking Ambassador Grew for American consent to these intentions, the Japanese minister had the effrontery to suggest that if "the American Government should at some later time decide to replace the *Panay,* the Japanese Government would appreciate receiving [the] contract for construction in Japan."[10] The answer was a diplomatically polite ignoring of the latter and a denial of the former relative to the *Panay.* The United States did acquiesce in the Japanese salvage of the barges on the understanding that Standard-Vacuum Oil Company representatives would be present and the books, documents, logs, and papers recovered would be turned over to the American consular authorities in China.

Not long after he had been given "liberty to leave Shanghai with his flagship at his discretion" Admiral Yarnell was in the middle of another controversy with the Japanese and the State Department. In June he announced to the American ambassador to China, Mr. Johnson, who promptly relayed the information to the Secretary of State, that he intended to visit Nanking and Wuhu about June 24 to 25 in the *Isabel.* How long he would be there depended on whether American nationals in the area needed assistance. After having asserted that he would give due notice of his movements to the Chinese and Japanese authorities and that he would take due care "to avoid unnecessary exposure in dangerous areas," he told the ambassador that the paramount mission of the U.S. Navy was to assist American nationals in the evacuation of such areas as Wuhu. The warning by the Japanese minister at large, Masayuki Tani, for foreign men-of-war to keep clear of combat areas did not, according to Admiral Yarnell, relieve "that nation in [the] slightest degree of responsibility for damage or injury to United States naval vessels or personnel." He would not even consider another suggestion by Minister Tani that United States naval vessels be painted scarlet or other colors to make them more distinguishable from the air. United States naval vessels on the Yangtze were the only ones of their type; they were painted white with large American flags painted on their awnings and that was identification enough.[11]

Whether Hull's reaction was due to the ambassador's message citing Admiral Yarnell's views or to the newspaper headlines over the United Press story dated Shanghai, June 12, is not known, but it was immediate. In a message back to Ambassador Johnson he quoted from the "sensational headlines" of June 13, such as: "Yarnell defies Japan"; "Says Navy will go where it is needed"; and "Won't bar U.S. ships in war zone." Hull pointed out again the public opinion against involvement in China and a growing insistence "upon the removal of all armed forces." Any suggestion of a bellicose attitude by Americans, official or unofficial, in China played into the hands of those opposed to an American presence. After having conferred with officers in the Navy Department, who had no indication of what motivated the proposed Yarnell visit, Hull questioned the advisability of the visit "at a time when active hostilities [were] imminent."[12]

He might well have been surprised by Ambassador Johnson's reply. Neither he nor Admiral Yarnell had given the press information on the visit. The ambassador suspected "that United Press was able to intercept the message which Yarnell [had sent] through naval wireless circuit and used it in its story." He personally saw "no reason why Admiral Yarnell should not make the visit contemplated." He felt there was no more risk of danger or embarrassment than visits to Tsingtao or Chefoo.[13] Admiral Yarnell elected not to go to the Wuhu area, but remained at Shanghai. History undoubtedly would have been more colorful had the Japanese river operations trapped Yarnell's flagship, the heavy cruiser *Augusta,* instead of the little gunboat *Monocacy.*

Second only to the *Panay* case in volume of messages, and perhaps exceeding it in the amount of resulting negotiations, was the incident involving the *Monacacy.* As the Japanese advanced up the Yangtze in the summer of 1938, the area of active fighting approached the city of Kiukiang where the *Monocacy* was located. Each of the key officials concerned with the *Monocacy* had evaluated her future safety relative to the Japanese advance. The Commander, Yangtze Patrol, Rear Admiral David McDougal Le Breton, after conferring with Ambassador Johnson and getting concurrence from Admiral Yarnell, had decided to leave the *Monocacy* in the vicinity of Kiukiang, though fighting was inevitable there.

Hull, on July 5, challenged the wisdom of the decision. He wanted to know how many Americans were in the vicinity and what were the future plans concerning the gunboat.[14] The immediate response from Johnson was that sixty American missionaries and businessmen in the area were "not casuals but persons with interests and property." They did not intend to leave their all to the Japanese.[15] Hull persisted. Back went another telegram to Ambassador Johnson via Frank P. Lockhart, the consul general, who was instructed to pass its contents to Admiral Yarnell also. Among other things, Hull said:

Would not giving by the *Monocacy* of notice of intended departure, with offer of transportation, lead to embarkation by such nationals as are willing to leave? Would any further standing by of the *Monocacy* serve any useful purpose in regard to those not willing to leave?[16]

The answers were sent to the State Department on July 12. The *Monocacy* was and would remain anchored in an open stretch of the Yangtze, "probably the safest place on the river between Kiukiang and Yochow at the present moment." The gunboat could not move upstream because the Chinese had heavily mined the river to stop the Japanese. Movement downstream was blocked by Japanese operations. Mr. Johnson pointed out that for months he, his staff, and the Navy had prepared for such a situation. The gunboats were "not interlopers in this area," and sooner or later they must pass through these hostilities or have the hostilities pass by them. The only course to follow then was to keep the Japanese completely and currently informed of the whereabouts of the vessels, insist upon the rights of noncombatants, and trust the Japanese "desire to do us no harm."[17]

Mr. Hull was not the only one who wanted the *Monocacy* moved upstream. On July 17, Ambassador Grew telegraphed from Tokyo that Japanese naval officials were quite worried over her presence near Kiukiang, and while they were taking every precaution to prevent the recurrence of another *Panay* incident, they could not cover all eventualities. Through Ambassador Grew it was requested that the gunboat be moved to Hankow. Acknowledging that such movement might be impossible due to mines or a boom, it was further requested that the ship be "especially marked or otherwise be made distinctly recognizable from afar and from high aloft."[18] There apparently was bona fide concern to prevent another *Panay* incident.

During the exchange of information and advice concerning the *Monocacy,* Mr. Hull received two other messages from different parts of China pertaining to relations between the United States and Japanese navies. On July 9, Consul General Lockhart at Shanghai forwarded to the Secretary of State a long statement which he had received from his Japanese counterpart. It was at once roses and thorns. The profuse gratitude was for "the hearty cooperation" the United States had shown by giving detailed reports concerning ship movements and avoiding areas of fighting in order to prevent incidents or casualties to life or property. This Admiral Yarnell had certainly done, whether or not it was completely of his own choosing. The stings of criticism, however, were definitely aimed at him, for they were over the issue of whether to make the gunboats more recognizable. He had continued emphatically to reject exotic paint schemes or other proposals to distinguish gunboats from other vessels on the river. The Japanese regretted that some powers considered "the flags printed on the awnings to be sufficient." Their pilots had found it impossible to distinguish flags without coming in "so low as to be greatly exposed to enemy anti-aircraft artillery fire." In addition, recognition depended on the relative position of the ship to the sun and how faded or soiled the flag had become.[19]

On the same day that Mr. Lockhart reported the Japanese consul's double-edged message, Mr. Samuel Sokobin, consul at Tsingtao, gave the final summary of an incident commencing on June 20. On that date Mrs. T. H. Massie, wife of Lieutenant Massie of the *Tulsa,* was slapped by a Japanese sentry on a pier in Tsingtao—even though she was being escorted at the time by two United States Navy enlisted men, one of whom was on shore patrol duty. Although the incident was reported to the American consul and notes were exchanged between Mr. Sokobin and his Japanese colleague, the two navies mutually smoothed over the repercussions of the event.

By coincidence, Captain R. F. McConnell, chief of staff, Asiatic Fleet, arrived in the *Augusta* on July 3 and immediately the Japanese chief of staff made an official call on him. He expressed the regrets of the Japanese Navy, admitted the actions of the sentry were unjustified, and sought ways to cooperate to prevent recurrence of such incidents and to settle them locally without reference to home governments. Captain McConnell accepted the apology, assured his visitor that the U.S. Navy would cooperate to prevent incidents of this kind, but pointed out that the present case was "being handled by the United States State Department" and that the United States Navy "had neither made nor received any communications with Japanese authorities in regard to the incident."[20]

Admiral Yarnell, in transmitting a summary of the discussions between the chiefs of staff to Mr. Sokobin, commented that it was "not exactly accurate to say that understanding had been reached between the American and Japanese authorities with regard to the final settlement of the case." However, since the Japanese naval authorities had shown a conciliatory attitude and appeared willing to cooperate to prevent recurrence, Yarnell could see nothing was to be "gained by continuing the controversy and that the incident should be considered closed."[21] Hull, probably pleasantly surprised to read such a report for a change, acquiesced in Yarnell's suggestion to consider the incident closed.

The presence of the *Monocacy* in the war zone, and the repeated suggestions by the Japanese to improve recognition techniques, prompted another communiqué to Ambassador Johnson, but it was meant as much for Admiral Yarnell as for anyone. Expressing his hope again that no unfortunate incidents would occur, Hull desired that intensive thought be given to the problems of operating naval vessels in the areas of fighting. His own words best describe his feeling of responsibility.

> I suggest that there be avoided express refusals to comply with Japanese and Chinese requests, suggestions or notifications; that if and when replies are made, their tone be made conciliatory; and that movements and operations of vessels be at all times such as to avoid fact or implication of being obstructive. I have neither authority nor desire to give commands regarding naval operations, especially at long range; but I am responsible in regard to the conducting of the foreign relations of the United States as a whole, and I am extremely solicitous that important efforts in other connections be not jeopardized by possible occurrence of unfortunate incidents in the local situation.[22]

Hull's telegram had just been sent when an incoming message, originated in Chefoo by Consul Quincy F. Roberts, reported the latest incident between the Navy and Japanese authorities. Intoxicated American sailors had assaulted four policemen and the Japanese chief of police. Preliminary investigation fixed the blame on the sailors and an acceptable basis for settling the matter had been worked out with the Japanese consul. On behalf of the Commander in Chief, Asiatic Fleet, Consul Roberts expressed regrets, promised that the naval personnel would be punished and that reimbursement for medical costs and torn uniforms, amounting to $55, would be made. During the investigation, however, a new incident occurred. The Japanese chief of police insulted Americans in general, the consul and senior naval officers in particular, and threatened them by flourishing an automatic pistol. This phase too was resolved by Mr. Roberts and the Japanese consul with the acceptance of a full apology from the bellicose chief of police in the presence of the ranking naval officers, the American consul, and puppet Chinese police officials.[23]

Roberts, who had acted promptly to settle the dispute locally, was criticized by his superior, the first secretary of the embassy in Peiping, Mr. Salisbury—first, for waiting five days after the incident before making the report; second, for acting on his own without prior approval of his seniors in the diplomatic system, and finally, for expressing the regrets of Admiral Yarnell which "would have more appropriately have been made by an American naval officer."[24] Fortunately for Mr. Roberts and future Japanese-American relations at Chefoo, Secretary Hull, Ambassador Johnson, and Admiral Yarnell all supported the actions of the consul. Yarnell came to his defense by asserting that Roberts had, in fact, cleared his actions with the Navy before agreeing with the Japanese to settle the matter locally. Johnson and Hull agreed with Yarnell that it was highly desirable to resolve minor differences locally. Again the Japanese diplomats appeared genuinely to want to maintain amicable relations with the United States.

On July 27, the *Monocacy* was present at the Japanese capture of Kiukiang in the course of which a Japanese gunboat approached the *Monocacy,* rendered honors, and departed back downstream. It was the last friendly gesture by the Japanese toward the *Monocacy* for weeks. The harbinger of future treatment came with a letter from the Japanese senior naval officer at Kiukiang denying the *Monocacy* permission to contact the American nationals in the Kiukiang area or to move the vessel to the Standard Oil installation nearby.[25] The next day the Japanese Navy representative at Kiukiang informed the commanding officer of the *Monocacy* that he would like to cooperate, but his orders came from the Army command at Nanking and future movements of the *Monocacy* were in the hands of higher authority at Nanking.[26] By this time Admiral Yarnell was very perturbed over the treatment of the *Monocacy;* little did he realize that much worse treatment was yet to come.

Since Admiral Yarnell was located in Shanghai and he wanted to communicate directly with the senior military commands in Nanking, he sent his messages through the *Oahu* at Nanking. Preferring to deal with the Japanese naval command rather than their army, Admiral Yarnell pointed out the obvious: the fighting was over and duty demanded that *Monocacy* officers promptly gain touch with American nationals and assist them in every way. The ship also required fuel. He requested that Admiral Koshira Oikawa, Commander, Third Fleet, issue the necessary instructions for the *Monocacy* to proceed to the Standard Oil installation by the end of the week.[27] The Japanese Army's authority over naval ships' movements was reemphasized in the answer to Yarnell's request. Rear Admiral Kusaga, the chief of staff of the Third Fleet, strongly objected to any shift of berth by the *Monocacy*, although he expressed sympathetic understanding of the desire to contact nationals and promised active cooperation to that end. He was unable, however, to forecast a date when such would be possible. Rear Admiral Nobutake Kondo reported on July 31 from Kiukiang that *Monocacy*'s movement from her berth to the city would interfere with Japanese operations and that consent of the army would have to be secured.[28]

On August 5, Commander Tanaga in Nanking informed the commanding officer, *Oahu,* that the Japanese Navy had no objection to the *Monocacy* berthing at the Standard Oil installation, but would not agree to her "doing so until permission had been obtained from General Shunroka Hata in Shanghai because of the previous 'unfortunate experience in Nanking,' "—the *Panay* sinking. The Japanese Army's answer was forthcoming. The *Monocacy* was refused permission to shift berth on the grounds that the new location would "permit close observation of their transports anchored in that vicinity and other military operations."[29] The United States Navy representative in Nanking made a strong protest against this attitude on the grounds that "we had no real interests in their military operations, were deeply conscious of our neutral status, and that their illogical objections to our reasonable request were incompatible with their repeated official protestations of respect for American rights and interests in China." Since they had allowed the *Monocacy* officers to contact the American nationals by letter, the Japanese Navy representatives in Kiukiang considered the matter settled except "to try to obtain permission from military headquarters for the *Monocacy* to . . . get fuel and then return to present anchorage."[30]

At this stage, Admiral Yarnell had almost exhausted the peaceful courses of action he could follow in the China area to get the Japanese to cooperate on the *Monocacy* question. On August 15, he called upon the Navy Department to seek the help of the State Department. It was necessary for the *Monocacy* to proceed to Shanghai on account of shortage of fuel and provisions and for relief of personnel. Yarnell stated that he was reluctant to bring about an incident by directing the *Monocacy* to proceed without Japanese consent, and he requested that the State Department take the matter up with Tokyo to secure permission for the passage to Shanghai.[31] The Secretary of the Navy immediately relayed Yarnell's message to the State Department for appropriate action. In instructions to the ambassador in Tokyo the American position on Japanese control of the Yangtze was spelled out by virtue of their possessing a captured boom across the river at

Matung. The Japanese claimed that because the boom was a prize of war, their control of traffic through the river naturally and legally followed. Hull told Ambassador Grew that the government of course could not "admit any such right or the validity of the basis invoked in support of that asserted right." Grew was directed to approach the Foreign Office to get the Japanese government to put an end to the "opposition of the Japanese military authorities" to the *Monocacy*'s passage to Shanghai.[32]

Both Hull and Grew still operated under the long-established basis of international relations that responsible governments either controlled or were held accountable for the actions of their military forces. They soon found out that, under existing arrangements in the government of Japan, the military commanders in China had the authority for ultimate decisions in the China area. A report of this development reached Washington on the same date via two routes. Ambassador Grew reported to the Secretary of State on August 19 that his efforts to obtain authority for the *Monocacy* to proceed to Shanghai had "proved abortive." He had been advised that it was the intention of the Japanese government not to intervene in the exercise by Admiral Oikawa of the discretionary powers vested in him. Having been thus rebuffed, Ambassador Grew took his case to the minister for foreign affairs and made strong oral arguments, basing his approach upon practical considerations and legitimate rights. He told the foreign minister that it was difficult to believe that the Japanese government "would leave entirely to the discretion of one of its subordinate officers the decision in a matter involving one of the primary rights of the United States." The foreign minister immediately consulted Admiral Oikawa, whose reply, relayed to Ambassador Grew, was that military operations precluded moving the *Monocacy* at the time, but that the Japanese Navy would provide logistic support to the gunboat until such time as it could be moved. Grew considered this "as a categorical refusal" and, while fully appreciating the seriousness of the issue involved, thought that there was no doubt but that he had "exhausted diplomatic resources."[33]

On August 19, Admiral Yarnell learned from Japanese naval sources in Nanking that decisions concerning the *Monocacy* would be made in China. Admiral Oikawa offered the same logistic support which the foreign minister had mentioned to Grew, but reiterated the previous objections to the gunboat's moving downstream. Admiral Oikawa emphasized to Admiral Yarnell that moving the *Monocacy* would interfere with Japanese strategy and tactics, that there was a danger of a chance mine, and that—because of possible mistaken identity—there was a danger of being fired upon by "excited Japanese gun crews." Finally, the Matung barrier was a prize of war and third powers had no more right to expect passage through it than they would have had if it remained an intact barrier under Chinese control.[34]

The attempts to put the negotiations concerning the *Monocacy* into the diplomatic system had failed and Admiral Yarnell's bargaining position was back to that of four days earlier with two new developments bearing on the situation. In the first, Admiral Oikawa's hand was strengthened considerably by the Japanese foreign office deferring ultimate authority to the Japanese military forces in China. Admiral Yarnell had no immediate countermove, since he had just exhausted the possibilities of diplomatic assistance in obtaining a clearance for the *Monocacy* to move. The second development was the assertion of cooperation and understanding by the Japanese admiral to Admiral Yarnell. Japanese restrictions on the freedom of movement had not changed; they controlled the passage through the boom at Matung in the river and in this case possession equaled ten-tenths of the law. The offer of Japanese logistic support had possibilities, and Admiral Yarnell recognized that the future of the *Monocacy* necessitated his cooperation with the Japanese naval commanders on the Yangtze.

The day after receiving the offer of help from Admiral Oikawa, Admiral Yarnell informed Admiral Leahy that, unless he was directed otherwise, he would reply to Admiral Oikawa and accept his offer. Without relinquishing any rights of freedom to navigate the Yangtze and recognizing the "special situation now existing below Kiukiang," he would delay sailing the *Monocacy* until a later date.[35] Admiral Leahy answered immediately that Yarnell's proposal was approved except for the acceptance of transportation of fuel and provisions from the Japanese. Also, the State Department recommended the words "in view of navigational difficulties" in lieu of "recognize special situation" which had been proposed originally.[36]

As the *Monocacy*'s fuel supply dwindled to its very end, Admiral Yarnell advised the Chief of Naval Operations, before informing Admiral Oikawa, "*Monocacy* must proceed Shanghai prior 10 September due shortage fuel and provisions request your view."[37] Yarnell had his answer the next day. He was to discuss with the Japanese command on the Yangtze "the necessity for the USS *Monocacy* to either proceed to Shanghai or to obtain coal from mill belonging to Anderson Myers, and that you very much prefer having the *Monocacy* proceed to Shanghai." At the same time it was suggested that an escort through the boom at Matung be requested. Admiral Leahy's suggestions were promptly passed via the *Oahu* to Admiral Oikawa.[38]

Admiral Yarnell's message setting September 10 as a deadline for the *Monocacy* to move down river motivated Admiral Oikawa, in a most unusual show of trust in Admiral Yarnell's integrity, to confide in the Americans the difficulties experienced by the Japanese in their river operations and to show the inconvenience of moving the *Monocacy* at the time. The Japanese had swept only a narrow channel between Wuhu and a point 15 miles above Kiukiang, in the process of which more than 700 mines had been destroyed and numerous casualties sustained by their ships. Below Kiukiang and at six locations pointed out on charts, Chinese detached units were very active. Above Wuhu it was necessary for all ships to proceed in convoys with a destroyer escort and all convoys were subject to sniping and indirect fire from Chinese field and heavy artillery located inland from the river. Congestion on the river was caused by the operation of hundreds of large ships and thousands of small craft. Their numbers presented a serious problem which would be complicated by the passage of even one small gunboat. In addition, passage down of the *Monocacy* would undoubtedly be followed by similar British demands for HMS *Cockchafer* and passage up of reliefs and ships of third powers. Admiral Oikawa believed the Japanese had never questioned the fundamental right of third powers to free navigation of the Yangtze but that the Japanese Navy did claim control of the passage through barriers by virtue of their capture and military nature.[39]

Admiral Yarnell, the following day, thanked Admiral Oikawa for the courtesies and frankness of his confidence and assured him that the trust would be respected. In view of Oikawa's consideration and friendly attitude, Yarnell was "willing to accede to his wishes and hold the USS *Monocacy* at Kiukiang for the time being."[40]

Meanwhile, in Washington, liaison between the working levels of the State and Navy Departments showed agreement that the Navy Department "would send no reply to Admiral Yarnell: In other words, the Navy Department would leave Admiral Yarnell free to accept the Japanese offer to transport mail, supplies, and possible personnel."[41] Yarnell did accept the Japanese offer to support the *Monocacy,* and on September 8 the flow of provisions upstream began from Shanghai. The first shipment of 16,000 pounds of naval stores, motion picture films, and mail was forwarded via HIJM *Steshio Maru.*[42] A few days later, HIJM *Azuchi Maru* departed Shanghai with sixty-eight packages of refrigerated provisions, ship's service and medical stores and one bag of mail.[43]

Coal continued to be a critical item. The *Oahu* was ordered to inform Japanese naval authorities that while periodic access to the Anderson Myers coal pile was "now permitted," *Monocacy* had no adequate equipment for the transportation of this fuel." The senior naval officer, at Kiukiang, agreed to deliver fuel but then stated that the navy had no facilities and was unable to arrange with the army to do so. "Request arrangements be made to supply the gunboat with coal of about 25 tons per week."[44] So coal was added to the shopping list of supplies being delivered by the Japanese.

In mid-September, one of the most interesting airlifts of the Sino-Japanese War took place. On September 14, a dozen sailors relieved from duty on the *Monocacy* were returned to Shanghai by a Japanese airplane provided by Admiral Oikawa. On September 24, two officers and thirteen enlisted replacements were flown in to Kiukiang, and on September 25, two officers and thirteen men relieved from duty on the *Monocacy* were returned to Shanghai by the Japanese plane.[45]

Further cooperation in Kiukiang was evidenced by a report from the *Monocacy* on September 26 that arrangements had been made with the Japanese Army for *Monocacy* to visit various missionaries to ascertain their needs and to explain the method of obtaining the same from Shanghai. All contact since August 6 had been by letter through the Japanese. The following day, two months after the Japanese had taken Kiukiang, a *Monocacy* officer, accompanied by a Japanese army officer and vice consul, visited Americans in the city. They were comfortable and, except for a scarcity of staples, there was no food shortage. The isolation of the *Monocacy* and the missionaries was over.[46]

The *Monocacy* episode pointed up a number of factors which would bear on future Japanese-American relationships over the Asiatic Fleet forces. First, the Japanese military forces in China were the ultimate authority on relations with third powers where military operations were involved. Second, the Japanese Army held higher authority than the Navy and was prone to be less cooperative with the Asiatic Fleet. Third, the Japanese were meeting unexpectedly stubborn Chinese resistance, which necessitated heavier Japanese effort than had been planned. Convenience to third powers would have a low priority. Finally, the Asiatic Fleet forces had to rely upon diplomatic representations to a government whose authority over its army in China was limited at best. The safety of American naval vessels and citizens and the security of property were in the hands of the Japanese military forces in China. In 1938 the Japanese still needed American oil, machinery, and iron for her war machine, so limited cooperation with the Asiatic Fleet was to their national interest. The understanding between Admiral Oikawa and Admiral Yarnell in the fall of 1938 was the high point of that cooperation.

While there might have been a flurry of cooperation in China with the Japanese Navy, there were also concurrent maneuverings within the United States Navy for possible better positions vis-à-vis the Japanese. Through the depression years the Japanese had been allowed to operate a very old transport, the *Mariana Maru,* in the copra trade in and out of Guam's only harbor. Since the administration of the island was a naval responsibility, the governor in July sought authority from the Navy Department to terminate the privileges of entry on September 30, 1938, the expiration date of the then current permit. The governor had information that, upon renewal of permission of entry authorization, the Japanese planned to replace the *Mariana Maru* with a bigger, more modern transport and to ask that the entry privilege be transferred to the newer vessel.

The Secretary of the Navy reviewed the Guam situation in the light of Japanese ship visits and United States defense requirements in a letter to the Secretary of State on July 28. The harbor at Guam had, by an Executive Order of September 23, 1912, been made a closed port to "any commercial or privately owned vessel of foreign registry [or] to any foreign national vessel, except by special authority of the United States Navy Department in each case." The Navy Department had approved the recommendation of the governor to revoke the privilege of entry of the *Mariana Maru* when the term of her permission expired. Admiral Leahy suggested that the Secretary of State inform the Japanese ambassador "that no action on his request to replace the *Mariana Maru* appeared necessary since the Navy Department [had] recently decided to close Guam to the entry of all vessels of foreign registry."[47]

The Hepburn Board studies contributed heavily to the actions by the Navy relative to the *Mariana Maru.* Congress, in May 1938, had directed the appointment of a board to survey the requirements for additional submarine, destroyer, minecraft, and naval air bases in the United States and its possessions. Rear Admiral A. J. Hepburn and his board were in Guam at the time of the initiation of the governor's letter. The Navy did not care to give the Japanese a ringside seat to view possible improvements in Apra Harbor. The board published its report on December 1, 1938. Pointing out concomitantly the defenseless position of Guam and its great potential, the board recommended that a strong air and submarine base be built there. With such a base, it reasoned, operations against the Philippines by Japan would be "a precarious undertaking"; extensive hostile naval operations to the southward would be impeded, if not denied, to Japan and "in time of sudden emergency Guam would provide for security of our Asiatic Fleet." The board's recommendations relative to bases in Alaska, Wake, Midway, and Oahu were eventually fulfilled, but, ironically, the first step in improving Guam as a base—a bill to authorize the dredging of Apra Harbor for submarines—failed to pass Congress.

In the fall of 1938 on the opposite side of the world, the threat of war in Europe grew heavier day by day. The German demands on Czechoslovakia in September, the ensuing Munich conference, and the hopeful "peace in our time" bought by Britain's Prime Minister Neville Chamberlain and France's Foreign Minister Edouard Daladier focused attention on Europe. The meteoric rise of Adolph Hitler in Germany had caught the war planners unprepared. The only current plan was the latest *Orange Plan* which, of course, related only to Japan. It was obvious to the planners that the European situation would increasingly bear upon the American strategic position. On November 12, 1938, the Joint Board instructed the Joint Planning Committee to make exploratory studies of practicable courses of action open to the military and naval forces of the United States "in the event of (a) violation of the Monroe Doctrine by one or more of the Fascist powers, and (b) a simultaneous attempt to expand Japanese influence in the Philippines."[48] Although the war planners would not finish their study until well into 1939, the product of their efforts would be the start of a new family of war plans to meet the vastly more complicated problem of multiple potential enemies hemispheres apart.

CHAPTER 4

British-American
Strategic Planning

The opening days of 1939 found the Japanese very much stalemated in their Chinese conquest drive. The seizures of Canton on the south coast of China and Hankow on the Yangtze in October 1938 were the last significant achievements. Chiang Kai-shek's withdrawal of the Nationalist capitol further upriver to Chungking irretrievably eliminated the possibilities of an early end to the war. The drain on resources and the loss of prestige by the Japanese Army gave the Japanese Navy the additional leverage it needed to gain concurrence in executing the next phase of the southward expansion policy.

On February 10, 1939, the Japanese occupied the island of Hainan off the coast of Indochina and nearly midway between Hong Kong and Singapore. As pointed out by Ambassador Grew at the time, possession of this strategic real estate enabled the Japanese to "check all traffic into and out of Hanoi," to control the South China Sea between China and Luzon in the Philippines, and to limit the "sphere dominated by Singapore."[1] The token objection by the French government, which had had an understanding with the Japanese that the status quo of the island would be maintained, was largely ignored.

While the Japanese were leap-frogging well to the south of their home islands, the United States House of Representatives debated and defeated an appropriation bill of $5 million to dredge Apra Harbor in Guam. Fear of appearing to be taking a stand against the Japanese prompted a number of votes against the bill. The isolationist tide in the United States then was very strong indeed.

Meantime, in Shanghai, the Japanese stepped up pressure on the municipal council to obtain control over the police matters in the International Settlement. A number of assassinations in the area gave the Japanese the excuse for demanding joint authority, ostensibly to control the terrorists. Admiral Yarnell, whose Asiatic Fleet command included the Fourth Marines at Shanghai, specifically ordered Colonel Joseph Charles Fegan, United States Marine Corps, not to enter into any agreement with the Japanese over sharing authority: "Either the commander of the Fourth Marines must have full authority or this force must be withdrawn entirely."[2] For the time being Japanese demands were ignored by the council. The International Settlement, because of the legal nature of the extraterritoriality of its component parts, was still considered American, British, Italian, and Japanese land. The French concession adjacent to the settlement was likewise considered part of France. The Japanese were not yet ready to take control of the national territory of such powers and certainly not all at the same time.

No such restraints deterred their annexing the Spratley Islands on March 30. These scattered bits of coral, located approximately 700 miles southwest of Manila, had been claimed by both France and Japan since the 1920s. Their strategic importance was that they afforded excellent anchorages for light naval forces and possible sites for airfields, but even more, they were midway between Hainan and Singapore—less than 700 miles from the most powerful British base east of Suez.

While the Japanese were moving southward, they were also pressing hard in Shanghai to test foreign reactions. On March 8, the Shanghai municipal police and the Japanese gendarmerie raided the American sector and arrested some Chinese without either American or council permission. Admiral Yarnell protested vigorously to the chairman of the municipal council, Mr. Cornell S. Franklin, who likewise protested to the Japanse consul general.[3] The American consul general, Mr. Clarence Edward Gauss, very adroitly kept the disputes within diplomatic channels. As the legal maneuverings continued it was apparent that, without any successes against the Chinese in the war, the Japanese were anxious to control commercial and financial interests in Shanghai and especially to deny to the Chinese the International Settlement as a haven from which to conduct their lucrative businesses.

In the spring of 1939, the United States Navy was involved in an unusual display of goodwill which came close to producing some undesirable results. Ambassador Hiroshi Saito had died in Washington at the end of February. As a friendly gesture President Roosevelt offered to make the heavy cruiser *Astoria,* commanded by Captain

Richmond Kelly Turner, available to transport Saito's ashes to Japan. The Japanese not only accepted the offer, but, trying to get maximum mileage out of the event, portrayed the visit as the start of a new era of understanding and friendship and as an approval of their policies vis-à-vis China. Lavish gifts and entertainment were planned for Captain Turner and his officers. It taxed the diplomatic ability of Ambassador Grew, with Secretary of State Hull giving advice from Washington, to decline, without offending, all but a tactful level of entertainment and participation by Captain Turner and his crew.

While Captain Turner was having an audience with the Japanese emperor, an interesting operation—especially in the light of latter-day relationships—was taking place on the Yangtze. On April 23, 1939, the Asiatic Fleet ships *Isabel* and *Oahu* departed Hankow, which had been in Japanese hands since the previous October, for Shanghai, taking twenty-four Americans, eleven Russians, four Swedes, and a Norwegian. The Russian contingent consisted of the counselor of the Soviet embassy, his wife, eight staff members, and a Tass journalist. The Japanese at the time were literally in control of all passenger traffic on the river since their commercial ships were the only ones moving freely up and down the river. In addition, foreign nationals had to get Japanese military "permission" to leave and to return to river ports even on naval vessels of their parent country. In previous weeks Grew and Hull had protested to the Japanese their controlling the movement of Americans, especially between Shanghai and Hankow where there was no fighting. In this particular move Admiral Yarnell had informed the Japanese admiral at Hankow of the identity of the Russian passengers, while the American, Swedish, and Norwegian consuls had identified their respective nationals to the Japanese consul general only so that their applications for passage on Japanese vessels might be withdrawn. Japanese authorities were not asked for permission to leave nor did they intimate that it was necessary. Evidently moves to Shanghai were acceptable since they were departures. On returns of Americans to Hankow and Kiukiang the consuls had to argue for each on a case-by-case basis with the Japanese consul general at Shanghai.[4]

In less than a month the Japanese were putting new pressures simultaneously on the International Settlements at Shanghai and Amoy. On May 12, at the insistence of the French consul general at Shanghai as head of the French concession, a joint proclamation was issued in conjunction with the chairman of the Shanghai municipal council. Its purpose was concomitantly to answer the Japanese complaints about Chinese "terrorist" activities in the foreign settlements and, at least in words, to serve notice on Japan that its own activities in the same areas would be controlled. The proclamation cautioned the "public that the neutrality of the foreign areas must be strictly respected and that unless political activity ceases immediately it will be necessary, without warning, to introduce strict curfew measures, and to expel all persons engaging in political activities." Finally notice was given by the French concession and the International Settlement administrators that they would take "the most drastic steps within their power to punish any person who at this time commits any act prejudicial to the preservation of peace, order and good government."[5]

Admiral Yarnell was quite concerned over possible Japanese reaction to the proclamation. He recommended to Admiral Leahy that the State Department notify the Japanese foreign office that "any unilateral action against the present Government of the International Settlement will be viewed with grave concern." Yarnell believed that the State Department should make public its notification to the Foreign Office "in order that the Nipponese Army will know, without being informed by their Foreign Office, of the views and attitude of the United States Government." This recommendation was made out of fear that the Japanese army "may take action without knowledge or approval of the Tokyo Foreign Office."[6] Hull did not publicize the decision to act on Yarnell's suggestion, but he did send instructions immediately to Grew to confer with the foreign minister on the subject. The foreign minister assured him categorically that "Japan had no intention whatever to occupy the International Settlement in Shanghai."[7]

On the same day that Admiral Yarnell requested the State Department to caution the Japanese against precipitously taking control of the International Settlement at Shanghai, the American consul at Amoy, Mr. Karl deGiers MacVitty, reported that the Japanese had landed 150 marines in the International Settlement at Kulangsu opposite Amoy. The next day, by coincidence, the Asiatic Fleet destroyer *Bulmer* arrived and two days later Captain John Taylor Gause Stapler, Commander, South China Patrol, Asiatic Fleet, arrived in the cruiser *Marblehead*. Admiral Sir Percy Lockhart Harnam Noble, in HMS *Birmingham,* with three destroyers, arrived the following day. For a show of joint strength, the American and British naval officers and consuls decided to land naval parties equal in number to the Japanese troops in the settlement. The French joined the show the following day with the arrival of a gunboat and subsequently landed a naval force equal in number to each of the others. Hull was perturbed over the landings and requested that the consul give him "by priority radio a statement setting forth how the landing of American naval units may contribute toward protecting American lives against excited and lawless elements," and to provide him with "more detailed daily radio reports than those thus far received."[8]

For the next five months a contingent of United States sailors and Marines, along with an equal number of Japanese forces, remained in Kulangsu, the British and French having withdrawn their forces to Europe after the commencement of hostilities with Germany in September. The persevering Japanese tried to coerce the municipal council into agreeing to turn over to them control of the police and administration of the council by cutting off food and fuel supplies from the mainland. It was truly a dress rehearsal in miniature for action in Shanghai. Diplomatic pressures by the British and Americans and a continued naval presence on the part of the United States, which allowed enough food to enter the International Settlement to negate the effect of the blockade, contributed immeasurably to the resulting impasse. Final resolution of the standoff occurred in October when the council reached agreement with the Japanese consul general to appoint one Japanese inspector of police, to suppress terrorists, and to hire ten additional Formosans as police at a later date. The day following the signing of the agreement, the Japanese and American forces were withdrawn simultaneously. In Kulangsu, as in Shanghai, the administrative rights of the council were protected, at least for the time being. The failure of the Japanese to carry their objective of complete control was due in no small measure to the collective action by the interested powers.

Cordell Hull, who was uncomfortable enough over the participation of American naval forces in the international confrontation at Kulangsu, was even more so when he read an Associated Press report on June 23 that eight American sailors from the destroyer *Pillsbury* were patrolling the entrances to the American Baptist Mission in Swatow. After giving his consul a lesson on the "Department's concept that naval units are landed for the purposes of protection of American citizens from individual acts of lawlessness and dangers incident to serious disorder," Hull asked for details of the landings. In identical language used on Mr. MacVitty at Amoy a month earlier, he also said he "would appreciate receiving if possible somewhat more detailed daily radio reports than those thus received."[9] A prompt reply to the Secretary of State told of several hundred panicky Chinese in the mission compound, a total absence of Chinese police protection, and insufficient Japanese protection to safeguard American property and citizens. The Japanese did not object at any time to the American landing force which was withdrawn in a few days, much to Hull's relief. No force had been necessary since the presence of American military strength alone was enough to restore order.

In June, while the international naval forces glared at each other in Kulangsu, the British were having second thoughts on long-range British-American naval force cooperation in the Far East. The assumptions which Admiral Leahy had passed to his fleet commanders for planning purposes in February 1938 were invalidated by events in Europe. The situation there had again drawn the major units of the British fleet to European waters. What would have been suspected by even an amateur strategist studying the deepening crisis in 1939 was confirmed by informal talks in Washington. The British naval attache, Captain L. C. A. St. J. Curzon-Howe, and Commander T. C. Hampton of the Admiralty met with Admiral Leahy and Rear Admiral Robert Lee Ghormley, chief of the War Plans Division in June. Commander Hampton, who was en route to duty in the Asiatic Station, had been sent to tell the Chief of Naval Operations that the situation in Europe and the Far East had changed so much during the past year-and-a-half that the Admiralty now had to give priority to the threat of Germany and Italy. If "Japan threatened, the British would not be able to send the force to the Far East that had been contemplated in the conversations with Rear Admiral Ingersoll."[10] This information was reaffirmed days later when Ambassador J. P. Kennedy reported from London on an all-day session of the cabinet on June 27 over the possibility of sending capital ships to Singapore as a threat to Japan for the humiliation of British subjects in Tientsin. The decision had been made in that case to weather the storm in Tientsin because the British fleet could not take on the Japanese and protect England against the German threat simultaneously.[11]

The British strategy, according to Commander Hampton, was "to maintain a portion of their Fleet in home waters and the remainder, except part of the China Detachment and the Dominion Forces, in the Eastern Mediterranean." In case of war in which Japan became involved, they would concentrate on Italy, the supposed weak link, and as soon as Italy was reduced, send naval reinforcements to the Far East. At the time, officers in the Admiralty were inclined to believe that Japan was less likely to join Germany and Italy than she was eighteen months earlier. Admiral Leahy informed his British visitors that he could not commit the United States Navy to any definite agreement, that he did not know what action Congress would take in case of trouble, nor could he discuss any action other than "parallel action." Leahy did say that the United States would undoubtedly send most of its naval forces to Hawaii in case of a European war in which Japan was involved and the United States was neutral.[12] Following the meeting, Admiral Leahy directed his fleet commanders to change their war plans to reflect the inability of Britain to send a large force to Singapore due to the world situation.[13]

A far-reaching move by President Roosevelt was made the following month. By issueing a Military Order on July 5, Roosevelt transferred the Joint Board into the newly established Executive Office of the President. The effect was that the Chief of Staff, Army and the Chief of Naval Operations were raised above their immediate civilian superiors and given a position of influencing national as well as service strategies. Roosevelt had earlier designated the two service chiefs to work directly with the under secretary of state in a standing liaison committee, which had been proposed by Hull to deal operationally with Latin American problems. The timing of these organizational changes was significant. The military service chiefs were in an unparalleled position to influence presidential decisions just before the start of war in Europe, just as new war plans were evolving and just as Admirals Leahy and Yarnell were being relieved as Chief of Naval Operations and Commander in Chief, Asiatic Fleet, respectively.

Meanwhile, the Japanese appeared to have taken a new tack in China during June and July. Having failed to crush Chiang Kai-shek's elusive armies, they launched a relentless campaign of bombing open, definitely non-military cities and hamlets, apparently to terrorize the Chinese people into submission. The effects were opposite to those desired—a stiffening of the will to resist and adverse world public opinion. As for the United States, there was more than public opinion involved. Concurrently, there was a marked increase in incidents of bombing of property, schools, and churches flying the American flag. On June 12 and again on July 6–7 bombs were dropped close aboard the USS *Tutuila,* and near the embassy office and embassy residential quarters in Chungking. After nonresponsive replies and inaction, even the pacific Cordell Hull had had enough. The President, Hull, and a unanimous Senate agreed upon the termination of the Treaty of Commerce and Navigation between Japan and the United States which dated from 1911. On July 26, Hull notified Japanese Ambassador Kemsuke Horinouchi that, according to the terms of the treaty, it would be ended six months later, in January 1940. The United States had finally taken a positive step—one which would allow economic sanctions to be used against Japan. The Japanese paused to weigh the significance but, in the absence of anything further, were not deterred from their course.

Through the early months of 1939, while the Japanese advanced southward to Hainan and the Spratley Islands and increased the tempo of activity against the International Settlements in China, in Washington the war planners of the Joint Planning Committee labored at reviewing plans in the light of the increasing German menace to the world. They presented their study in April, five and a half months after receiving the directive. The decision of the British to concentrate naval forces in Europe to check the Germans and Italians was a difficult one to make, for it meant weakening their position against the Japanese at a time when strengthening that position was the order of the day. The American war planners, in a more limited sense, found themselves in the same position. If the Western Hemisphere were to be defended against a rising German and Italian threat, naval forces would have to be used because they were the only existing military force. Force to be used in the Western Hemisphere could not be used against Japan also and a one-ocean navy could not be spread around the world and be effective.

The war planners concluded that Germany and Italy could violate the Monroe Doctrine by supporting Fascist revolutions in Latin America. The relegation of such countries to the status of colonies would give to their European exploiters the advantages of trade, access to raw materials, and military and naval bases. From such bases the Panama Canal possibly could be attacked. Finally, the planners discounted the possibilities of German or Italian action in Latin America unless: (a) Germany believed that Britain and France would not intervene and (b) Japan moved to attack the Philippines and Guam and even then only in case the United States had responded to the Japanese attack by counterattack in the western Pacific.[14]

However, to overcome glaring deficiencies in existing war plans concerning concerted action by Germany, Italy, and Japan, the Joint Planning Committee recommended that future plans reflect new possibilities. That recommendation received immediate approval and action. In less than three weeks, four of a new family of tentative plans were offered to the Joint Board for approval. The most limited plan, *Rainbow 1*, provided for the defense of the Western Hemisphere south to the bulge of Brazil, 10° S. Two other plans provided alternatively for the extension of operations from this area: *Rainbow 2*, to the western Pacific, and *Rainbow 3*, to the rest of South America. *Rainbow 4* envisaged Great Britain and France at war with Germany and Italy and possibly Japan, with the assumption that the United States would be involved as a major participant.

Reexamination of the possibilities under *Rainbow 4* led the planners to the conclusion that if all the major powers were at war using their current forces, operations in Latin America would probably be very limited in scope whereas operations by Japan in the Pacific would probably be extensive in scope. The recommendation was made that there be two plans covering United States participation with Britain and France against Germany, Italy, and Japan. One plan provided for the United States to furnish armies for a maximum effort in Europe against Germany and Italy, while the other plan called for not providing maximum effort in Europe, maintaining the Monroe Doctrine, and carrying out "allied Democratic Power tasks in the Pacific." The Navy by that time, June 1939, had completed talks with the British over cooperation in the Pacific against the Japanese and unofficial agreements had been reached. The joint planning committee recommended that the plan for the United States to concentrate war effort in the Pacific be moved up in priority to the *Rainbow 2* position where it might "conceivably press more for answers" than plans other than *Rainbow 1* would. Part of the justification for the change in priority read:

> Whether or not we have any possible intention of undertaking a war in this situation, nevertheless we may take measures short of war, and in doing so should clarify the possible or probable war task that would be involved.[15]

A week later, on June 30, the Joint Board approved the recommended change in priority. The revised description of the new five *Rainbow* plans read:

1. To prevent violation of the Monroe Doctrine, and to protect the United States, its possessions, and its sea trade.

2. To carry out No. 1, and also to sustain the authority of democratic powers in the Pacific zones.

3. To secure control of the Western Pacific.

4. To afford hemisphere defense, through sending U.S. task forces if needed to South America, and to the eastern Atlantic.

5. To achieve the purposes of 1 and 4, also to provide ultimately for

sending forces to Africa or Europe in order to effect the decisive defeat of Germany or Italy or both. This plan assumed U.S. cooperation with Great Britain and France.[16]

With the definitions of strategic objectives having been clarified, the Joint Planning Committee had the basis for all future planning until the United States entered the war in December 1941. Shifting emphases in the priority of developing the five *Rainbow* plans resulted from changes in the international situation. All the plans in one way or another had a bearing on the two plans against Japan, *Rainbows 2* and *3*.

As should be expected, the security of the Western Hemisphere received first priority. *Rainbow 1* was submitted to the Joint Board on July 27, 1939, where it was studied, slightly changed, and submitted directly to President Roosevelt in accordance with his Military Order of July 5; he approved the plan orally on October 14, 1939.

On August 14, while the plan was before the President, Admiral Harold Raynsford Stark, who had become Chief of Naval Operations on August 1, sent to Sumner Welles, under secretary of state, a secret memorandum relative to the political aspects of *Rainbow 1*. He believed it was necessary that Welles should read it for background information, but felt that since it quoted joint basic war plans it should be destroyed or otherwise protected after it had been read. This was an opening move for future close personal relations between Admiral Stark and Mr. Welles. Part of the secret memorandum read:

> ... The *General Situation* under which these plans are being prepared is as follows: Germany, Italy and Japan, acting in concert, violate the letter and spirit of the Monroe Doctrine. Japan, supported by Germany and Italy, violates by armed aggression vital interests of the United States in the Western Pacific. It is to be assumed that aggression initiated by one or two of these powers will be eventually supported by the concerted action of all three.[17]

The next priority after *Rainbow 1* applied to *Rainbows 2* and *3*, the two Pacific area plans. "The Joint Board had directed the Joint Planning Committee in June to give priority to the development of plans for United States naval offensive in western Pacific (*Rainbow 2* and *3*) in the event of war with Japan."[18] Even after war began in Europe a few months later, the strategic thinking continued to emphasize the plans against Japan. Since Britain and France controlled the Atlantic, and to a lesser degree the North and Mediterranean Seas, the most likely action to involve the United States in war would be an attack by Japan in the Pacific. Planning for such an eventuality was much more complex than planning for *Orange* plans in the past. Not only were other "democratic powers" involved in the Pacific, but additional potential enemies who might act in concert existed in the Atlantic.

Another problem facing the planners was how far the Japanese would advance and in which direction before the United States and the "democratic powers" could take action. The navy planners of the joint planning committee set up three alternative hypotheses:

- Japan had not begun to move southward from Formosa. The United States Fleet might move to Manila Bay with detached units to Singapore, Cam Ranh Bay, and Hong Kong with ground troops either accompanying or following later to the western Pacific. These acts hopefully would prevent a war in the Pacific.

- Japan had already taken Hong Kong and Cam Ranh Bay and had begun operations in the Netherlands Indies. In this case the United States would react by moving forces to the Far Pacific, whereupon the Japanese would move against Guam and the Philippines.

- Japan had already taken the Netherlands Indies and isolated Singapore and was in a position to take the Philippines. The Army planners on the committee pointed out the obvious: in this case "the principal advantage of Allied participation will have been lost and the problem becomes essentially that of an *Orange* War."[19]

The last hypothesis was most prophetic, considering it was two and one-half years in advance of the actual performance. Only the inability of the planners to fathom the lurking vulnerability of Singapore to land attack marred a classic prophecy.

A bit of the color left the China scene when Admiral Yarnell was relieved by Admiral Thomas Charles Hart on July 25, 1939. A few days before being relieved, Admiral Yarnell sent the Secretary of the Navy his evaluations of the effectiveness of American foreign relations in the Far East and his military recommendation for strengthening the hand of the diplomat. He observed that, during his tour in China, the rights of Americans in the Far East had been "upheld vigorously by the State Department," and the position and policies of the United States could not have been stated more clearly or more positively. On the other hand, Yarnell thought the Tokyo government was generally impotent to deal with or give decisions regarding affairs and incidents in China, because in many cases it was entirely ignorant of what was going on there. Then the admiral offered the advice which he would consistently repeat until war came, namely:

> ... that for every note written, there should be some increase in the United States armed forces in the Far East. When dealing with a nation whose policies are determined by a ruthless military clique which worships the sword and understands nothing but force, such a procedure may have merit.[20]

Just days before war commenced in Europe, Admiral Stark received advice from two different directions relative to his policy toward Japan. His own staff in the War Plans Division observed that in the event Britain and France entered war against Germany, "the invitation to aggression by Japan in the South China Sea Area would prove so promising that [it] ... would be hard for that country to resist even if they so wanted." Without suggesting how to do it, the war plans staff thought "that the United States [should] take immediate steps as may be practicable to provide a deterrent effect against such aggressive measures by Japan."[21]

The next day Admiral Yarnell gave Admiral Stark, the new Chief of Naval Operations, the benefit of his experience in the Far East. In language reminiscent of similar advice given to Admiral Leahy a year before, Admiral Yarnell volunteered that:

1. We should never engage in a war single-handed against Japan if at all possible. Great Britain, France, and the Netherlands are vitally interested and should take part.

2. In case of a single-handed war, we cannot move our fleet to Eastern waters due to lack of a base.

3. I do not believe our government will ever build a first class Naval base in the Philippines.

4. We can never compete with Japan in transporting U.S. troops to the Far East.

5. The war should be a Naval war,—cruisers, submarines, and aircraft operating against lines of communications.[22]

Admirals Stark and Hart and the War Plans Division would attempt right up to the start of war to develop and put into operation plans encompassing Yarnell's perceptions.

Meanwhile, in China, the Japanese lost no time in exploiting the European war to their advantage vis-à-vis the British and French. On September 5, the Japanese government informed the European belligerents that the continued presence of their warships and troops in China "might result in unfortunate incidents and in a condition of affairs ill adapted to Japan's 'non-involvement policy'."[23] Consequently, Japan gave them "friendly advice" to withdraw these forces voluntarily and offered to undertake the protection of the lives and property of their citizens.

Secretary Hull learned of the Japanese action from two sources. Consul General Gauss in Shanghai reported that the British and French military there had told Admiral Hart of the squeeze, while in Washington the British and French diplomats had sought advice and support from Hull. On September 7, Hull did see the Japanese ambassador and told him that although his government was trying to force the Western powers out of China, American troops would remain there. He also implied that the congressional proponents of economic reprisals might have their way. That was all he could or would do. On September 11, he advised the British to make no reply but "to keep them guessing."[24]

In Shanghai, Admiral Hart took the position that *any* change in the nature of the International Defense Plan definitely affected his forces and a full revision of the plan with United States representatives participating would have to be made before any change was consummated. The International Defense Plan, made originally in 1931 and amended in 1934, was an agreement among the commanding officers of the British military forces, the U.S. Fourth Marines, the Japanese naval landing party, the chairman of the Shanghai Municipal Council, the commandant of the Shanghai Volunteer Corps, and the commissioner of the Shanghai Municipal Police, with the commanding officer of the French military forces accepting the plan—as long as it made provision for cooperation and mutual aid between the French forces and the forces of the International Settlement. As far as the Western powers were concerned it was a military rather than a diplomatic agreement.

At a September 14 meeting of defense commanders, the Japanese commandant in Shanghai urged a revision of the defense plan "pointing out that it was originally intended to protect foreign nationals from the Chinese and that this necessity no longer existed."[25] The participants agreed to submit the matter to a committee to draft proposals. Neither at this meeting, at another on September 23, nor at a showdown on November 14 did the Japanese bring up the issue of British or French withdrawal. In the November meeting, the Western military leaders took the attitude that if there could be no agreement among them it would be best to await the results of diplomatic efforts before proceeding further. One reason the Japanese were not pushing for British withdrawal from Shanghai was that Britain had withdrawn five gunboats from the Yangtze and cut her garrisons in Peiping and Tientsin to token levels sufficient only to preserve her rights under the Boxer Protocol. Through the rest of 1939, France and Italy also drew down their respective forces in Peiping and Tientsin to a mere handful at each legation and, like Britain, France withdrew its gunboats from the Yangtze River. As 1940 approached, only the United States had maintained former force levels in North China and on the Yangtze.

CHAPTER 5

The
Rainbow War
Plans

Shortly after Admiral James Otto Richardson broke his flag as Commander in Chief, United States Fleet, in the battleship *Pennsylvania* on January 6, 1940, he received a letter from Admiral Stark, Chief of Naval Operations, pointing out that events in the Far East might "be far more important to us than the troubles in Europe, especially if something should break and break quickly and without warning."[1] It was, Stark told Richardson, "something ... for which you should be mentally prepared." Stark also indicated that Admiral Hart, Commander in Chief, Asiatic Fleet, thought that the situation in the Far East was serious and that the year 1940 "may prove to be a crucial and critical one." It was apparent that the senior naval commanders in Washington and China were more concerned at the start of 1940 over the explosive potentials in the Far East than in the lingering standoff in the European war.

Richardson did not completely share the concern of Stark and Hart. First, he was not pleased with the fact that a large detachment of the fleet, consisting primarily of cruisers and destroyers, had already been sent to Hawaii. Now he found Stark's comments on something breaking without warning and being mentally prepared "somewhat disquieting." In a letter dated January 26 Richardson outlined his views on the naval role in national strategy and especially relative to Japan. He told Stark that as assistant chief of naval operations he had constantly pushed Admiral Leahy, then CNO, to impress upon the President that "we do not want to be drawn into this [the China incident] unless we have allies so bound to us that they cannot leave us in the lurch." He estimated that war with Japan would last five to ten years and cost 35 to 70 billion dollars. He evaluated the *Orange Plan* as good only as a training device for war planners and as a basis for asking for appropriations. The Navy needed time and money to develop bases for the fleet "to put on any real pressure" and "should not go into a thing like this unless we expected to see it through."[2] Richardson would reiterate many times the value of a trained and supplied fleet based on the West Coast rather than one without proper logistic support, based in Hawaii. Doggedly, he urged his position on Stark, and later on President Roosevelt, until he was finally relieved by Admiral Husband Edward Kimmel in February 1941.

In answer to a letter of March 8 from Richardson asking why there was a Hawaiian detachment of cruisers and destroyers, Stark reviewed the requests of the previous fall from Admiral Hart that the Asiatic Fleet be reinforced with a division of heavy cruisers, or if they were not available, light cruisers. The situation in the Shanghai area at the time of the request was very tense; war had commenced in Europe and the Japanese were becoming increasingly more belligerent toward the British on the Yangtze and in Shanghai and Tientsin. The State Department and the President agreed with Stark to send the cruisers only as far as Hawaii, and to reinforce the Asiatic Fleet with one tender, a squadron of patrol aircraft, and six new submarines. Stark favored leaving the detachment in Hawaii indefinitely, because "no one can measure how much effect its presence there may have on *Orange* foreign policy." The State Department, according to Stark, strongly supported his deterrent concept.[3]

On March 31, 1940, American newspapers carried the news that the annual fleet exercises would be held in Hawaiian waters. In 1935, the last time the exercises had been held in that general area, American pacifists had led the claim that such an act was hostile to Japan. This time the exercises were kept to an area well eastward of the 1935 exercise area, yet the Japanese newspapers were filled with accusations that the exercises were threatening. Despite the Japanese attitudes the fleet left West Coast ports on April 2 and conducted Fleet Problem XXI in the Hawaiian area.[4] While the United States Navy exercised in fleet war games, the German war machine suddenly came to life. After an immediate occupation of Denmark on April 9, the Germans invaded Norway and defeated a spirited though weak British attempt to hold northern Norway.

Meanwhile, in Washington, the war planners continued their

work on the *Rainbow* family of plans. One of the hypotheses the Navy planners used as a basis for *Rainbow 2* was that the Japanese had seized Hong Kong and begun operations against the Netherlands East Indies. On the possibility that the start of the German spring offensive might be paralleled by Japanese actions, the Joint Board on April 10 "directed the Joint Planning Committee to proceed immediately with the completion of plans for an immediate projection of U.S. forces into the Western Pacific."[5] The initial movement of forces was planned for Singapore and the Netherlands East Indies, to be supported, if the hypothesis held true, across the Atlantic, by way of the Cape of Good Hope and Indian Ocean. To insure that Singapore would be available to the U.S. Fleet, the Navy recommended that the British be asked to send a division of capital ships to reinforce their naval forces in the Far East. It was further recommended that the British, Dutch, and French authorities be contacted diplomatically to ascertain their proposed actions in the Pacific vis-à-vis Japanese aggression. Another explosive political question was whether United States forces would be used to defend the European colonial possessions.[6] Before these questions could be answered, events in Europe turned attention away from the Pacific for the time being.

While the war planners worked on *Rainbow 2,* Admirals Stark and Joseph Knefler Taussig, a previous assistant chief of naval operations, testified before the Senate Naval Affairs Committee for more appropriations for the Navy. Taussig created quite a furor in Japan by asserting that war with Japan was inevitable. Despite a special press conference by Secretary of State Hull and denials by Navy Department spokesmen to the press that Taussig's statements were his own opinions and not the government's, the impact in Tokyo was considerable. Naval attaches reported from Tokyo that evidently strict orders had "been issued to Japanese officers not to discuss either naval matters or relations with the United States. Friends of many years duration refused to speak of Admiral Stark's and Admiral Taussig's testimony in front of the Senate Committee and declined to comment on same even in informal conversations."[7]

On May 7, Stark wrote a hurried letter to Richardson, who was at Pearl Harbor with the fleet after the exercises. He had "just hung up the telephone after talking with the President" and wanted to explain in more detail by letter the order sent by dispatch "to remain in Hawaiian Waters for a couple of weeks." Richardson was told that when the fleet returned to the West Coast ports, he was to keep enough fuel and stores aboard all ships so that on short notice it could return to Hawaii *en masse*. The primary concern on May 7 was whether or not Italy would enter the war against Britain and France and trigger a move by Japan against the Netherlands East Indies. Stark called the "Italian situation...extremely delicate, the two weeks ahead regarded as critical."[8]

The next move in Germany's blitzkrieg came suddenly and soon. The Chamberlain government fell on May 10 over dissatisfaction with the British performance in the Norwegian campaign. On the same day, Winston Churchill became Prime Minister and Germany turned its juggernaut against the Netherlands and Belgium.

In Hawaii, Richardson chafed at tying the fleet to the inadequate base at Pearl Harbor. He considered the assumptions upon which past plans had been based to be completely different in the light of the deteriorating European situation. On May 13 he wrote to Stark:

> It seems that, under present world conditions, the paramount thing for us is the security of the Western Hemisphere. This, in my opinion, transcends everything—anything certainly in the Far East, our own or other interests.
>
> South America is the greatest prize yet remaining to be grabbed...

He added that any move to the west meant hostilities and would be a grave mistake since U.S. interests there were not vital. The ability of the fleet to protect the Western Hemisphere should not be reduced; however, if higher authority decides that "we should go west, all of us are ready to give all we have." In an interesting postscript to the letter, Richardson told Stark that he had sent a detachment to simulate a raiding force against Pearl Harbor to test the efficiency of Navy patrol planes and Army bombers. The Navy planes had seen the group, but the Army bombers had not.[9] In the spring of 1940 at least one admiral was thinking about the possibility of an attack on Pearl Harbor.

The Netherlands government, on May 14—after four days of fighting which included the devastating bombing of Rotterdam—surrendered to Germany. The next day Churchill, referring to himself as a "Former Naval Person," wrote to President Roosevelt of the seriousness of the situation. His list of immediate needs to fight the war against Germany was almost all-inclusive, except manpower. He wanted

> First of all, the loan of forty or fifty of your older destroyers to bridge the gap between what we have now and the large new construction we put in hand at the beginning of the war. This time next year we shall have plenty. But if in the interval Italy comes in against us with an-

other one hundred submarines, we may be strained to the breaking point. Secondly, we want several hundred of the latest types of aircraft, of which you are now getting delivery. These can be repaid by those now being constructed in the United States for us. Thirdly, anti-aircraft equipment and ammunition, of which again there will be plenty next year, if we are alive to see it. Fourthly, the fact that our ore supply is being compromised from Sweden, from North Africa, and perhaps from Northern Spain, makes it necessary to purchase steel in the United States. This also applies to other materials. We shall go on paying dollars for as long as we can, but I should like to feel reasonably sure that when we can pay no more, you will give us the stuff all the same. Fifthly, we have many reports of possible German parachute or airborne descents in Ireland. The visit of a United States Squadron to Irish ports, which might well be prolonged, would be invaluable. Sixthly, I am looking to you to keep the Japanese quiet in the Pacific, using Singapore in any way convenient.[10]

Eventually everything on the order was filled, with the glaring exception of the use of Singapore and visits to Irish ports.

After the fall of the Netherlands, concern within the Navy Department over expected Japanese moves into the East Indies reached a fevered pitch. In retrospect, it appears that the officers in the War Plans Division, in particular, were grasping at straws in desperation to counter the expected southward advance. On the day Churchill wrote to Roosevelt about his needs, Captain Russell Sydnor Crenshaw, chief of that division, convinced Admiral Stark that certain of the proposals from the planners should at least be taken up with the State Department and the President. One proposal was that, if the Japanese Navy moved into the area of the Netherlands East Indies, that the United States Navy make similar moves—or, an interesting variation on that proposal, that the U.S. Navy participate in "courtesy calls" *with* the Japanese, by sending a division of *Omaha*-class cruisers to the East Indies to be under the operational control of Commander, Asiatic Fleet, for as long as needed.[11]

With Admiral Stark's approval, the chief of the Central Division, OpNav, Captain Roscoe Ernest Schuirmann, visited the Far Eastern Division of the State Department on the same day, May 15. There he discussed with Dr. Hornbeck and Mr. Hamilton the proposals "that if Japan sends a small occupation force for the protection of the Dutch East Indies" that the United States send a similar force, or, that the United States should "suggest or notify Japan that if they occupy the islands that the United States share in the occupation." Hornbeck and

Hamilton were in positive agreement that unless the United States "were prepared to go to war, if necessary, in the event such a joint occupation were opposed by Japan that [the United States] should not make such a move." The proposal of suggesting to Japan some joint occupancy would not be feasible according to the diplomats, since Japan had already stated that it wished the status quo preserved in the East Indies. Schuirmann explained that these were merely suggestions that the Navy was exploring and the reactions of the State Department to them was desired "in order to clarify our own ideas."[12] Now, having gotten the reactions from Hornbeck and Hamilton, the navy proponents abandoned the ideas.

Nevertheless, the Joint Army and Navy Board recognized that the United States was the only power in a position to restrain the Japanese from taking action in the Netherlands East Indies. In connection with the studies of possible cooperation with the Allies, the naval attache in London, Captain Alan Goodrich Kirk, was instructed by the board just before the Netherlands fell to obtain full information as to facilities that might be available at Singapore for a naval detachment, should the United States decide to support British and Dutch resistance to any further Japanese move to the south.[13] The Admiralty expressed a strong desire "that the United States Government guarantee the Netherlands East Indies."[14] On May 17, Kirk reported an Admiralty proposal that the United States send naval forces to Singapore. Admiralty staff officers pointed out that, if the Japanese moved southward for any reason, they could easily cut British lines of communications between Australia and India.[15]

Meanwhile, from the Far East came a report that Japan too was in the dark over Italy's future moves. On the day the Netherlands capitulated, First Secretary Robert L. Smyth in Peiping reported to Secretary Hull that the Japanese in Peiping were "displaying keen interest in regard to the question of Italian entry into the European war." The analysis of the United States attaches and Smyth was that the Japanese would again request the "belligerent powers to withdraw their armed forces from China as in September last."[16] Unknown to the diplomats were concurrent actions being taken by Admiral Hart to get an "agreement between the European forces in Shanghai to maintain the peaceful status quo." The informal oral agreement reached among the senior military commanders of the European powers was accomplished "without consultation with . . . civil authorities." Admiral Hart thought that the Italians in Shanghai were "fully disposed to keep their word, even though there [were] signs that their local civil authorities [were] rather put out over the Italian commander's having entered into the agreement." By design, the agreement was reached without knowledge of the Japanese, although they were informed after the fact. Hart thought the effect on them was "even amusing." He wrote Stark:

> ...our move caught the local Japanese authorities quite flat-footed and they have been trying to recover from the surprise and to answer criticism from their own higher-ups ever since. Our initiative in the matter was, I am sure, a very good and profitable move. An incident between white troops which the Japs could call disorder would give them just the pretext which they may be looking for.[17]

Secretary Hull, having learned about the agreement made in Shanghai, furnished the details to Ambassador Grew in Tokyo. In addition, he advised, "the commanders of the detachments of European forces at Peiping have manifested a completely cooperative attitude in keeping with the agreement reached at Shanghai, and that the United States Government assumed that the agreement included the detachment at Tientsin also." Grew was told to inform the Japanese Foreign Office that the United States expressed satisfaction with the development.[18]

On May 22, Admirals Richardson and Stark each originated a letter to the other. In Stark's previous letter of May 7, he had mentioned to Richardson that the "Italian situation is extremely delicate, the two weeks ahead regarded as critical." Now on May 22 Stark admitted to Richardson that two weeks earlier "it looked as if Italy were coming in almost immediately and that a serious situation might develop in the East Indies and that there was a possibility of our being involved." However, the recent blitzkrieg events in Europe had certainly altered the picture for the time being. Stark thought events had made "more remote [for the moment, at least] the question of a westward movement of the fleet." Although the possibility was remote, planning for such an eventuality was going full speed ahead. Stark told Richardson that *Rainbow 2* was nearing completion and would be sent to him by officer messenger as soon as possible. Richardson was instructed "to go ahead with the preparation of a tentative Fleet Operating Plan for *Rainbow 2*," but to keep "constantly in mind the possibility of a complete collapse of the Allies, including the loss of their fleets." Such a catastrophe was considered in *Rainbow 1*. Should the Allied fleets pass into the hands of the Germans, however, an entirely different, and far more serious situation would exist. Richardson was asked to give his views regarding the best disposition of U.S. fleet forces in such an event. In a postscript Stark indicated the pressures of his job. He wrote:

> Have literally lived on the Hill—State Dept.—& White House for last several days. Thanks God yesterday I finally swung support for 170,000 men and 34,000 marines.[19]

Admiral Richardson's letter of May 22 was his most perceptive in the series exchanged with Stark. The fleet was still in Hawaii—past the "couple of weeks" it was to have stayed after the fleet exercises. He pointed out to Stark that since he had to plan the fleet schedule and employment for the next few months he had to know more about why the fleet was there and how long it would remain. Even curtailed gunnery training would require wholesale movement of targets, tugs, drones, and utility aircraft. Richardson then asked two most poignant questions:

> (a) Are we here primarily to influence the actions of other nations by our presence, and if so, what effect would the carrying out of normal training . . . have on this purpose? . . .
>
> (b) Are we here as a stepping off place for belligerent activity? If so, we should devote all of our time and energies to preparing for war. . . .
>
> As it is now, to try and do both (a) and (b) from here at the same time is a diversification of effort and purpose that can only result in the accomplishment of neither.

At the end of his letter Richardson pleaded with Stark to push for more enlisted men, to operate the training stations at full capacity, and to train men as quickly as possible in order to fill the complements of new ships being built and others being recommissioned.[20]

While Richardson's letter was enroute to Stark, the highest council in Washington again reviewed the war plan situation in the wake of the German victory over the Netherlands and in the face of the impending fall of Belgium and possibly France. The President, Under Secretary of State Welles, Army Chief of Staff General George Catlett Marshall, and Admiral Stark on May 23 agreed that "we must not become involved with Japan, that we must not concern ourselves beyond the 180th Meridian, and that we must concentrate on the South American situation."[21] Work was suspended on the two plans involving Japan, *Rainbow 2* and *3*, but evidently only by the Army. After years of having worked on the *Orange Plan*, the navy planners were not ready to write off the Philippines and Guam. They continued to

61

work on *Rainbow 3* throughout the fall of 1940, and not until August 6, 1941 were *Rainbow 2* and *3* cancelled.

In line with the May 23 agreement the Joint Planning Committee gave top priority to *Rainbow 4*—the defense of the Western Hemisphere. The purpose of the plan was:

> To provide for the most effective use of United States' naval and military forces to defeat enemy aggression occurring anywhere in the territory and waters of the American continents, or in the United States, and in United States' possessions in the Pacific westward to include Unalaska and Midway.[22]

Rainbow 4 was finished the end of May and forwarded by Secretary of War Harry H. Woodring and Acting Secretary of the Navy Lewis Compton to the President on June 13.

The evolution of the strategic thinking in Washington in the spring of 1940 made Stark's answers to Richardson's what-are-we-doing-here letter all the more interesting. The agreed-upon emphasis, as of May 23, was upon the defense of the Western Hemisphere, and not to become involved with Japan or actions west of 180° longitude. Yet on May 27 Stark answered the question as to why the U.S. Fleet was in Hawaii:

> You are there because of the deterrent effect which it is thought your presence may have on the Japs going into the East Indies. . . . Along the same line as the first question you would naturally ask—suppose the Japs do go into the East Indies? What are we going to do about it? My answer is that . . . , I don't know and I think there is nobody on God's green earth who can tell you. I do know my own arguments with regard to this, both in the White House and in the State Department, are in line with the thoughts contained in your recent letter.
>
> I would point out one thing and that is that even if the decision here were for the U.S. to take no decisive action if the Japs should decide to go into the Dutch East Indies, we must not breathe it to a soul, as by so doing we would completely nullify the reason for your presence in the Hawaiian area. . . .
>
> You ask whether you are there as a stepping off place for belligerent activity? Answer: obviously it might become so under certain conditions but a definite answer cannot be given as you have already gathered from the foregoing.
>
> I realize what you say about the advantages of returning to the West Coast for the preparation at this time is out of the question. If you did return it might nullify the principle reasons for your being in Hawaii. This very question has been brought up here. As a compromise,

however, you have authority for returning ships to the Coast for dock-
ing, taking ammunition, stores, etc., and this should help in any
case. . . .[23]

Richardson was also given permission to curtail or to change the
scheduled gunnery exercises in any manner he saw fit. He was reminded again that, should the situation change in the Atlantic, some
ships from the U.S. Fleet at Pearl Harbor would be ordered to the
Atlantic. Stark's reading of the situation on May 27 was that the force
so ordered would not be extensive—"a division of cruisers, a carrier,
a squadron of destroyers, possibly a light mine layer division, possibly
Patrol Wing One, and possibly, but more unlikely, a division of submarines with a tender." He closed with another estimate of Italy's
entering the war in Europe—June 5.[24]

A side issue arose at the same time Stark issued his guidance to
Richardson over possible movements to the Atlantic. It was minor, in
retrospect, but indicative of the pressures on the President, the inter-
relationships of the requirements for naval forces in the Pacific and
Atlantic Oceans, and the influence Stark had with the President. The
United States minister to Uruguay, Mr. Edwin C. Wilson, was deeply
concerned about open and very active Nazi propaganda efforts in
Latin America, especially in Uruguay. Fear of a coup along the lines
of successful tactics just used in Norway generated one message of
panic after the other. To counter the German moves as he foresaw
them, Wilson proposed that the United States send—as a one-time
show of force—forty or fifty ships to the South Atlantic and then leave
a powerful squadron along the eastern coast of South America indefinitely. Roosevelt's immediate response was to order the heavy
cruiser *Quincy,* then at Guantanamo, Cuba, to Montevideo, the capital of Uruguay, and to refer the matter to Stark for advice. Meanwhile, Under Secretary Welles argued for much heavier forces than
just the *Quincy*—at least three or four cruisers and a reasonable number of destroyers.[25]

Stark, in a memorandum of June 2, reviewed the defense problems and in the Western Hemisphere ended with the immediate solu-
tion to Wilson's and Welles' request for more forces. He wrote:

I offer the following solutions:—
(a)   Dispatch one additional 8″ cruiser to South America.
(b)   Continue destroyer shakedown cruises to South America.—
(c)   If desirable at a later date;—Reinforce the above by another heavy
      cruiser and/or a squadron (9DD) of destroyers.

(d) For the present utilize ships now in the Atlantic, thus not weakening the fleet in the Pacific....[26]

Roosevelt passed the Stark memorandum to Welles the following day with a covering memorandum which read:

Please read enclosed from Admiral Stark sent me last night, Sunday. Stark is absolutely right and gives in paragraph #13 the only solutions possible.[27]

Stark did send another heavy cruiser, the *Wichita,* to join the *Quincy* and the crisis came to a head and passed with the actions of the Uruguayan congress on June 13 dissolving all "illegal organizations." Stark had not had to touch his Pacific forces.

From the Asiatic Station Admiral Hart, on June 7, reviewed his first ten months of duty there. He observed that delays in moving the gunboats still continued, caused in almost every case by requests from the Japanese Navy made at the insistence of the Japanese Army. Two months before, he had reported on the problems that Rear Admiral William Alexander Glassford, Commander, Yangtze Patrol, was having with the Japanese over getting clearance to move U.S. gunboats from place to place. At that time Hart admitted that giving in to the Japanese so often "irked him considerably" but that he "would risk [his] personal reputation as long as the respective cases . . . in themselves [were] unimportant." He did not want to have "an *incident* over something which did not amount to much, per se." Now in June Glassford wanted to relieve the gunboat at Hankow. After two months of postponements by the Japanese Navy, Hart decided to put his foot down. A threat to report the delays to Washington induced cooperation on the proposed gunboat trip to Hankow. Hart told Stark that it was obvious to him that the Japanese "Army and Navy in Central China did not want any discussions of [delays] by the respective capitols . . ." Hart's self-evaluation of his record for the first ten months was that in every instance he had had his way "though quite frequently having to delay a bit to get it."[28]

On the same day Hart wrote Stark about the comparatively peaceful relations with the Japanese, the American consul in Canton received from his Japanese counterpart a letter charging the United States Navy with a violation of international law on the high seas. Four destroyers were reported to have ordered a Japanese military transport, HIJM *Shinko Maru,* to heave to off the South China coast near Amoy at longitude 118°13' East and latitude 23°54' North on May 7 at 8:05 A.M. (The destroyers were Destroyer Division 59—the

Pope, Peary, Pillsbury, and *John D. Ford.*) After four months of exchanging notes through diplomatic channels at Canton the incident was termed a misunderstanding. Through examination of the deck and signal logs of the destroyers involved and conferences with United States naval officers, it was determined that a small International "K" flag was being flown as a tactical signal just high enough above the bridge of each ship for the adjacent ships to see it. It was not flying at the yardarm and it was not displayed with the "International Code" pennant necessary to make it the international signal to heave to as read by the Japanese commanding officer. The destroyers had passed the transport on an opposite course at least one mile to starboard. They had not made a run in on the transport and then veered away after signalling, as alleged. The investigative report by the Commander in Chief, Asiatic Fleet, was either acceptable to Japan or it effectively checkmated the initial allegations, since no further action was taken by the Japanese consul general at Canton. The incident differed from previous cases involving the two navies in two significant ways: (a) This time it was Japan who initiated the complaint; and (b) the complaint, until resolved, was handled in proper diplomatic channels rather than between military commanders directly, as in the Yarnell era. It was just one year after the *Monocacy* incident.[29]

Admiral Hart had written on June 7 that he had gotten his way with the Japanese military in China in every instance though having to delay at times a bit in doing so. The prognosis for relations between other occidental powers and Japan appeared much less favorable in the event Italy entered the war. Rear Admiral Walter Stratton Anderson, the director of naval intelligence, reported to Admiral Stark on June 8 that he had "thoroughly reliable information" that if Italy entered the war Japan would take the following actions in China:

(a) Use force to remove or disarm the European belligerents' forces in China if any fighting occurs between them.

(b) Reissue the warning of 5 September 1939 to France and Britain regarding maintenance of peace and withdrawal of armed forces.

(c) Issue the same warning to Italy, after first confidentially informing her and negotiating and arranging for withdrawal of Italian troops on condition that France and Britain evacuate.[30]

As events developed in China in the summer of 1940 the assessment proved to be quite accurate.

Despite Japanese anticipation of trouble among the European belligerents, the relationships worked out by Admiral Hart to continue the status quo peacefully were successful in every quarter. In Tientsin British, French, and Italian commanders agreed on June 11, the day after Italy entered the war, to avoid friction. The Italian concession was "out of bounds" to British and French liberty parties. All other concessions were to be open to all nationals except that military personnel were to be in civilian clothes and military vehicles were to fly no flags. Any incidents between European troops were to be resolved by the senior United States Marine Corps officer present.[31] Very much the same arrangement was made in Peiping the following day. Liberty would be on alternate days for Italian and Anglo-French enlisted men with certain places of amusement "out of bounds" and the senior commandant present to be the arbitrator of any disputes.[32] Since the senior commandant was Marine Colonel Allen Hal Turnage, the "keeper of the peace" at Peiping, as in Tientsin, was an officer who reported to Admiral Hart. By August, after the French-Italian armistice, the commandants of the French and Italian embassy guards had reached a supplemental agreement to lift the restrictions on alternate-day liberty in Peiping. By the end of August when the supplemental agreement was signed, there were in Peiping on duty with the embassies only two French officers and 15 men, one Italian officer and 36 men, and nine British men.[33] There were fewer European troops yet in Tientsin, while U.S. Marines numbered sixteen officers, a warrant officer, and 315 men in Peiping and thirteen officers, a warrant officer, and 225 men in Tientsin.[34] In Shanghai, cooperation among the European powers paralleled that in Peiping and Tientsin; however, Japanese pressures to force out the British and French were more persistent and successful in the latter part of June.

In Washington the collapse of France caused more concern than any other foreign event at the time. President Roosevelt gave his hypothesis of the war situation in the fall of 1940—six months in the future—to Rear Admiral Anderson, director of naval intelligence, and to Brigadier General Sherman Miles, director of military intelligence, for their evaluation. Roosevelt foresaw that Britain and the British Empire would still be intact; that the French government and surviving French forces would still be resisting in North Africa; that British and French navies, in conjunction with the U.S. Navy, would control the Persian Gulf, Red Sea, western Mediterranean, and the Atlantic from Morocco to Greenland, having probably been driven out of the eastern Mediterranean; that Japan and Russia would not be active in the war but that the United States would be active, though with naval and air forces only.[35]

The intelligence chiefs, who received the President's hypothesis on June 13, turned for recommendations as to how to answer to the War Plans Divisions of their respective services. Colonel Frank S. Clark and Captain Charles Johnnes Moore, the senior Army and Navy members, respectively, of the Joint Planning Committee wrote a report to the Chief of Staff and Chief of Naval Operations entitled *Views on Questions Propounded by President on War Situation.* They took exception, in part, or completely, to each of Roosevelt's forecasts. They thought that Britain, as distinguished from the British Empire, would probably not "be an active combatant" in six months. Likewise, they reasoned that France could not continue to resist in North Africa since she would be cut off from supplies, weapons, and ammunition there. The war planners had information that Japan and the Soviet Union on June 9 had settled a longstanding dispute over the border between Manchuria and Outer Mongolia and they read this as an omen that not only would the two enter the war, but that they might take concerted offensive action in the Far East. Roosevelt's forecast of naval strength appeared reasonable to the planners with the exception that the situation in the Mediterranean would be the reverse of that foreseen by him. The last item, that the United States would be active in the war, really disturbed the planners. The limited arms production in 1940, a one-ocean navy, presidential insistence that munitions be furnished Britain at a time when American requirements were increasing—in contrast to a desire to deter Japan from further aggression in the Far East—all made the assumption that the United States would be an active participant within six months seem dangerous to the planners. They urged their superiors to discourage the President from getting the country involved as a belligerent before it was adequately prepared. They spelled out what would probably happen if the United States entered the war prematurely:

> Belligerent entry by the United States in the next few months would not only disperse and waste our inadequate means, but would result in leaving the United States as the one belligerent to oppose the almost inevitable political, economic, and military aggression of totalitarian powers.
>
> Early entry of the United States into the war would undoubtedly precipitate German subversive activities in the Western Hemisphere, which we are obligated to oppose. Our ability to do so, or to prepare Latin American countries to do so would thus be ham-strung.
>
> Our entry into the war might encourage Japan to become a belligerent on the side of Germany and Italy, and might further restrict our efforts on behalf of the Allies.[36]

The report was never sent to Roosevelt. It was overtaken by events of

June 17 and a subsequent study originated by the Navy on June 22, which incorporated most of the expressed ideas and ultimately became, on June 27, a document entitled *Basis for Immediate Decisions Concerning the National Defense.*

The day of June 17 certainly was one of the busier days in 1940 for decisions, actions, and the commencement of significant events. Early in the morning (2:00 A.M.) Ambassador Anthony J. Drexel Biddle reported from Bordeaux, the temporary capital of France, that a new French government—formed just the day before under Marshall Philippe Petain—had asked Germany for armistice terms. Fear that the French fleet might surrender to Germany was so strong that Roosevelt, the day before, had urged the French government through its ambassador, Count St. Quentin, to continue the war from North Africa or at least to send the fleet to British ports. News of the request for armistice terms increased fears of Germany getting the fleet and triggered further American actions later in the day.

Later in the morning of June 17, by coincidence, naval intelligence reported that, should Germany and Italy gain control of the French fleet, their combined naval strength would be about one-third greater than the British fleet and greater also than the U.S. Fleet, most of which by design was in Hawaii. The same report pointed out that with the French fleet at his disposal Hitler had a much better chance of a successful invasion of Britain.[37]

The potential disparity in naval strength also bothered Mr. Churchill. On June 15 and again on June 17, he repeated his request for thirty-five destroyers. On May 15 he had requested forty to fifty destroyers. All the requests went unanswered for the time being because there did not seem to be a legal way to make the transfer and the Navy Department insisted that they could not be spared.[38]

On the same day, again by coincidence, Roosevelt sent a request to Congress for new construction for a two-ocean navy. The Navy General Board had already proposed that the United States Navy be expanded drastically so that it would be dominant in both the Atlantic and Pacific Oceans. The Roosevelt request on June 17 was for 1,300,000 tons of new shipping. The belated start of the race for naval supremacy was on, just eighteen months before many of the existing capital ships would be sunk or damaged at Pearl Harbor. In budget terms, the amount made available by Congress for contract authority in fiscal year 1941, which began two weeks later, jumped to $946,098,-112 from $22,450,000 the previous year—a level almost forty-three times higher. Increased personnel, training, and base support expenditures necessary to man the new construction likewise increased. Total appropriations approved by Congress for fiscal year 1941 for the navy rose to 3.5 billion dollars. The previous year the appropriations were only 0.9 billion dollars.[39]

Three other actions taken by Roosevelt on June 17 followed relative to the French situation. First, he ordered a freeze on all funds of the French government. Since France had already transferred most of her gold stocks to the United States for safekeeping and had also deposited funds to pay for heavy defense contracts for aircraft and ammunition, the funds frozen were considerable. Second, Roosevelt—in anticipation of favorable congressional action—served notice that European possessions in the New World could not be transferred as a result of the war. By joint resolution on June 17 and 18 the Senate, unanimously, and the House, 380–8, so voted. Roosevelt sent notes to Germany and Italy, with information copies to Britain, France, and the Netherlands of the United States' stand on hemispheric integrity.[40]

The last action again concerned the French fleet. Late in the afternoon (5:00 P.M.) a note, which Secretary Hull himself described as "almost a brutal message,"[41] was telephoned to Ambassador Biddle at Bordeaux to be passed to the French government. Churchill, who had requested Roosevelt to intercede with Petain not to surrender the French fleet, had sent a parallel message in much more diplomatic language and had received Petain's answer that he could not send the fleet to Britain, but that Germany would not get it and, if necessary, it might be scuttled. Ambassador Kennedy's telephone call from London at 7:00 P.M. concerning this information arrived too late to stop the instructions given Biddle. Biddle was told, among other things:

> The President desires you to say that in the opinion of this Government, should the French Government, before concluding any armistice with the Germans fail to see that the Fleet is kept out of the hands of her opponents, the French Government will be pursuing a policy that will fatally impair the preservation of the French Empire and the eventual restoration of French independence and autonomy. Furthermore, should the French Government fail to take these steps and permit the French Fleet to be surrendered to Germany, the French Government will permanently lose the friendship and goodwill of the Government of the United States.[42]

In reply, French Foreign Minister Paul Baudouin told Biddle that the last sentence of the Roosevelt message "deeply pained" the French government, but assured him that the fleet would never be surrendered, but that it might be sent overseas or sunk.[43]

Two separate items of intelligence originated from Tokyo on June 17 to intensify even more the confusion and coloring of the kaleidoscopic situation of that day. One was to presage further Japanese activities in the Pacific, while the other was to meld with additional bits of intelligence and cause an immediate reaction in Washington affecting United States forces in the Pacific. On June 17 (possibly on June 18), the Japanese director of military intelligence told the British military attache in Tokyo that "the Japanese people would be cowardly if they failed to take advantage of the opportunities presented by the disasters suffered by the French and British. Nothing could stop Japan from seizing French Indo-China, the Netherlands Indies, or Hong Kong—any or all of them." Britain could avoid war only by closing the Burma Road and the Hong Kong frontier and by prompt withdrawal of British troops from Shanghai. These blunt forecasts became realities when formal demands along these lines were made of Britain on June 24 and June 27.[44]

The other intelligence item was from Ambassador Grew. To understand its significance better, other intelligence reports which preceded it should be examined. On May 27, Japanese newspapers published an official note from Germany to Japan giving Japan carte blanche to take control of the Dutch East Indies. On June 3, Ambassador Grew sent a long five-section message analyzing the future actions of the Japanese government and the increasing rivalry between the three major factions: the pro-German, pro-Russian, and the pro-democratic groups. The country was in a "state of political turmoil of unusual intensity." The pro-Russian militants, made up of reactionary societies and younger army officers, planned to overthrow the existing government by autumn. They advocated a partition of China along Polish lines and then an immediate "seizure of the Netherlands East Indies before a German victory in Europe would give Germany a similar opportunity." They discounted the possibility of war with the United States and believed that in any case "the Japanese fleet had nothing to fear from the use of force." Germany, meanwhile, was exploiting its European successes to gain support among its followers in Japan. Their plan was to intensify anti-American demonstrations so that "the United States will be less prone to enter the European War against Germany." The pro-democratic group was the least vocal and politically most vulnerable of the three groups. The crux of the June 3 message was found in Grew's words: "... a complacent view of the future would no longer be warranted."[45] On June 10, Japan and the Soviet Union had reached a rapprochement in settling the Manchukuo border dispute. On June 14, the Japanese-sponsored Wang Ching-wei government in Nanking demanded the recall of British, French, and Italian troops and warships from China.

In addition to the preceding chronology, the Office of Naval Intelligence acquired two additional bits of unsupported information that influenced the evaluation of the June 17 message from Grew. On May 1, there was a lead that German sabotage of the Panama Canal was planned and on June 13 there was a report from a Brazilian crew that Japanese ships would be scuttled in the canal if the United States mobilized. The preceding items were all bits of a mosaic taking on particular characteristics before June 17. With the Grew message the mosaic was complete—at least to the War Department officers. In the context as they read it, the United States was in imminent danger.

Grew's message to the Secretary of State originated from Tokyo on June 17, was received in Washington during the evening of June 16–17, due to the time difference, and was passed almost immediately to the naval and military intelligence offices. In the War Department General Marshall and his top advisers held a conference at 8:30 A.M. June 17 to discuss the international situation in light of the Grew message, which read:

> Confidential reports have been coming to us from various sources of considerable concentration of Japanese military forces in Hainan, Formosa and Kyushu, but these reports are not subject to confirmation. Soviet and British attachés here are speculating with regard to a possible Japanese invasion of French Indo-China in the event of the capitulation of France in Europe.[46]

In reviewing the "various possibilities" General Marshall remarked that the United States "may suddenly find Japan and Russia appear as a team operating to hold our ships in the Pacific." Then he speculated on the effect of the French navy going to Germany and Italy: "...we will have a very serious situation in the South Atlantic. Germany may rush the South American situation to a head in a few weeks." During the conference Marshall favored "a purely defensive action in the Pacific, with a main effort on the Atlantic side." To this end they unanimously recommended bringing the fleet to the Atlantic. If this were not possible, then they asserted the need for additional long-range bombers to patrol the approaches to the Hawaiian chain, because "opponents in the Pacific would be four-fifths of the way to Hawaii before we knew that they had moved."[47]

Later in the morning General Charles D. Herron, Commanding

General, Hawaiian Department, received the following message from the War Department:

> Immediately alert complete defensive organization to deal with possible trans-Pacific raid, to greatest extent possible without creating public hysteria or provoking undue curiosity of newspapers or alien agents. Suggest maneuver basis. Maintain alert until further orders. Instructions for secret communications direct with Chief of Staff will be furnished you shortly. Acknowledge.[48]

A similar message was sent to the Commanding General, Canal Zone.

Admiral Stark sent no such message to Richardson, who at the time was aboard the fleet flagship *Pennsylvania*, in Lahaina Roads, Maui. In fact, Stark apparently sent no message to any naval commander paralleling the Army alert or even telling them that the Army had called an alert. Years later Stark testified that he "was not impressed so far as the Navy was concerned, with any particular gravity at that time." He "looked on it largely as an Army affair."[49] It is possible that Stark had a fixation on getting the fleet to the Atlantic and saw no reason to alert the commander about an enemy to the west when the fleet was going to be moved to counter another enemy in another ocean. Already he had ordered some ships from Hawaii to the Atlantic in anticipation of Germany gaining the French fleet. On June 18 by note he urged Roosevelt to return the fleet to the Atlantic. In this he had the complete support of Welles and Marshall with whom he had discussed the matter on June 17. Roosevelt delayed his answer. Stark sent Richardson a message to take the fleet out of Hawaii on or about June 24, after having leaked that the destination was the Canal Zone. The objective was to test the report that "any movement in force by major Fleet units toward Atlantic will occasion extensive sabotage in Canal." Richardson was told the Army in the Canal Zone was on alert, but no mention was made of the alert in Hawaii. After proceeding toward the canal for two days, maintaining radio silence, he was to return the fleet to Hawaii and to anticipate coming to Washington for a conference.[50]

What to do with the United States Fleet was the question of the day on June 18. Marshall and Welles agreed with Stark that it should be brought to the Atlantic to deter German action and to protect South America. Churchill, through his ambassador, Lord Philip Ken Lothian, had found support in Dr. Stanley K. Hornbeck, who was Secretary Hull's chief adviser on affairs in the Far East. The British reasoned that as long as the British fleet could control the eastern

Atlantic, it was an advantage to deter Japan by naval force in the Pacific—and the corollary to that, if the fleet withdrew from Hawaii, Japan would feel free to do whatsoever she wanted in the Pacific, thereby aggravating the international situation all the more. Should the British Isles become untenable, the British had indicated that their fleet would proceed to Singapore and *then* the United States Fleet could move to the western Atlantic and the Caribbean Sea. Roosevelt on June 18, when urged by Stark to move the fleet, did not know what to do and is reported to have said to Stark: "When I don't know how to move, I stay put."[51] On June 24, he told the navy that the "decision as to return of the Fleet from Hawaii is to be taken later."[52]

In the immediate wake of the June 17 decisions Roosevelt made two major changes in his cabinet. At some point in time during the preceding two or three months Roosevelt had decided to run for an unprecedented third term as president. With an eye to the future workings of the government as it geared for war, and certainly with an eye to the elections in the fall and to gaining bipartisan support should the United States enter the war, he brought into his cabinet on June 19 two prestigious Republicans. Colonel Frank Knox, editor of the *Chicago Daily News* and unsuccessful vice presidential candidate in 1936, was named Secretary of the Navy, while Mr. Henry L. Stimson, was named Secretary of War.

Both Knox and Stimson were much more vocal on foreign policy recommendations than the President could afford to be at the time. In fact, both had made major speeches on June 18, the day before they were appointed to the cabinet. Knox in Detroit had advocated compulsory military training, an army of one million men (In June 1940 the army strength was 230,000 men and 13,500 officers.), either the building of an enormous fleet or close cooperation with the British to control the Atlantic, and the construction of the most powerful air force in the world, providing as many planes as possible to Britain. Stimson's speech in New Haven paralleled that by Knox. He too was for compulsory military training, for opening U.S. ports to the British fleet for repairs and servicing, and for the United States Navy to convoy supplies and munitions to Britain.[53] These two activists were Roosevelt's kind of men and complemented his cabinet ideally for his wartime needs.

On June 22, Richardson and Stark each originated letters to the other. Stark's short letter to Richardson said that his trip to Washington "was held in abeyance because of uncertainty as to movements of the fleet in the immediate future." Richardson had planned to return to the West Coast on May 9 after the fleet exercises. After he had been ordered to remain in Hawaiian waters "a couple weeks," Stark had written his why-are-you-in-the-Hawaiian-area letter on May 27. In the order to execute a feint toward the Canal Zone Richardson had been told to anticipate coming to Washington upon his return with the fleet to Hawaii. Now in the latter part of June he was again being told "to stay put." Tentatively, the decision had been made for the fleet to remain where it was, but the decision was conditional, based on what happened to the French fleet.[54]

Richardson's letter to Stark on June 22 was a much longer one than he had received. In it Richardson reviewed how he, as Commander in Chief, United States Fleet, with his fleet in Hawaii, had received the information about the June 17 army alert. General Herron, upon receipt of the War Department message alerting the army forces in Hawaii had asked Rear Admiral Claude Charles Bloch, Commandant, Fourteenth Naval District, who was also Commander, Base Force, for help in long-range patrols against "possible carrier and plane attacks." Bloch informed Vice Admiral Adolphus Andrews, Commander Scouting Force and the senior officer present afloat (SOPA) at Pearl Harbor, about the request for patrol assistance. Richardson, Commander in Chief, U.S. Fleet, was at the time in the *Pennsylvania* in Lahaina Roads, Maui. When he was told about the alert and patrols, he asked Bloch by dispatch whether the request for "additional air patrol" was "part of an army exercise" or was "it based on information from the War Department." Bloch's answer was that the request by Herron "was based on a directive from the War Department." Herron had no information as to whether or not it was an exercise. Since Herron did not know and none of the admirals had the slightest hint as to what was going on, Richardson flew back to Pearl Harbor and, after conferring with his subordinates and General Herron, he sent a dispatch to Stark on June 22.[55]

> Commanding General Hawaiian Department received orders War Department placing forces on alert against hostile trans-Pacific raid and since no information received Navy Department have assumed this exercise. Navy patrol planes are participating.[56]

Stark replied by priority dispatch:

> War Department directive concerning alert issued as precautionary measure after consultation with Navy and State Department. Request you continue cooperation.[57]

Richardson closed out his letter of June 22 by observing that "the Army 'alert' and action caused" him some concern though he was "positive that any Army intelligence bearing on the above would be available to and evaluated by the Navy" and that he would be provided with this information. Since "anything of this character tends to aggravate the tenseness of the situation and to interrupt training" and a "serious situation may again arise," Richardson offered the Chief of Naval Operations the following advice:

> ...a remedy would be to insure that where possible, when joint action is involved, even in drills, that the Commanders of the Army and Navy be jointly informed, with definite information to me as to whether the alarm is real or simulated for the purposes of training.[58]

In Washington, on the same day as the Richardson-Stark exchange, the draft of *Basis for Immediate Decisions Concerning the National Defense* was discussed by Stark, Marshall, and Roosevelt. After the oral review Roosevelt ruled on the question of returning the fleet from Hawaii. That decision "would be taken later." The rest of the draft needed revision—a task given to the Joint Planning Committee. On June 27, Stark and Marshall presented Roosevelt with the revised edition which incorporated the Roosevelt comments of June 22. The recommendations for the immediate future were:

> (1) a defensive position by the United States; (2) nonbelligerent support of the British Commonwealth and China; (3) hemisphere defense, including possible occupation of strategic bases on the soil of Allied Nations' western colonies in case of those nations' defeat; (4) close cooperation with South America; (5) speeding of production and training of manpower, including a draft act and "progressive" mobilization; and (6) preparation of plans for the "almost inevitable conflict" with the totalitarian powers, to assure concerted action with other nations opposing Germany, Italy, and Japan.[59]

Each week which passed without German invasion of the British Isles made the strategy of June 27 look more attainable, and through the summer and into November when Admiral Stark wrote his *Plan Dog,* it was the strategy followed.

As the military leaders of the United States were presenting their commander in chief with strategy guidance, Japan was presenting the final in a series of demands forecast earlier by its military intelligence director. On June 24, Britain was asked to close the Burma Road to war materials and other goods and to take similar action relative to the Hong Kong frontier. To make their point that they meant business,

Japanese forces in China massed 5,000 troops on the Kowloon border —the strip of British territory on the China mainland immediately opposite Hong Kong. The move on June 27 was an additional demand that British troops leave Shanghai.

The demands of June 27 prompted the British ambassador, Lord Lothian, and the Australian minister, Mr. Richard G. Casey in Washington, to ask Secretary of State Hull for help in standing up to the Japanese forces in China. Lothian pointed out that since the collapse of France, Britain alone was having to fend off Japanese demands. Would the United States either join in an embargo or send ships to Singapore to show a cooperative front against Japan, or, if not, would the United States join Britain in mediating a peace settlement between China and Japan. Hull's answer to all items was negative. "Sending the fleet to Singapore would leave the entire Atlantic seaboard, north and south, exposed to possible European threats. Our fleet is already well out in the Pacific, near Hawaii." "As to the embargo proposal, we have been progressively bringing economic pressure on Japan since last summer..." Concerning making peace with Japan, the United States had nothing to offer Japan in the way of concessions or assistance and "no properties or interest of China should be offered to Japan by Britain or the United States. In other words, we do not make peace with Japan at the expense of China..."[60] At this stage there was no help in the offing from the United States for the British in the Far East. The British maneuvered for time, but by July 14 had worked out an agreement to vacate Shanghai, to close the Burma Road for three months during which time they would work towards a Sino-Japanese peace agreement.

The same bitter medicine experienced by the British was forced on the Vichy French. Japan also asked France to close the border of Indochina next to China and to withdraw its forces from Shanghai. Ambassador St. Quentin asked Under Secretary of State Sumner Welles for help in Indochina since additional demands included the admission of Japanese agents to inspect imports and exports to insure compliance by the French. He received no satisfaction. When Welles was asked then if the United States was interested in taking over the French concession in Shanghai, his answer was that the United States "would make no commitment of any character to the French Government at this time with regard to this question."[61] The recent failure to get France to move its fleet well out of the reach of Germany was still fresh. There was no thought of helping the French in Indochina now.

Admiral Hart on June 25 had recommended, in the event that the British and French troops were forced out of Shanghai, that the United States at least take over the Defense Sector B, controlled by British forces, which contained the American Consulate General and numerous other important American interests. Hart was willing to concede to Japan the British Defense Sector D, the second of two being vacated by the British, if U.S. Marines could control Sector B. At that time in Shanghai the Marines numbered 47 officers, 7 warrants, and 1,011 men.[62]

On August 9, Britain announced that her forces would be withdrawn from Shanghai, Tientsin, and Peiping. Immediately thereafter, Colonel DeWitt Peck, commanding the Fourth Marines, requested a meeting of the Shanghai Defense Committee on August 12. Representatives from British, French, American, and Italian forces, Shanghai Volunteer Corps, and the municipal police attended. The Japanese command, apparently waiting for instructions from Tokyo, did not send a representative, but by letter requested another meeting on August 15. At the August 15 meeting the proposal made by Colonel Peck that Japan take over Defense Sector D and the United States take over Sector B was approved by a majority vote. Only the Japanese voted "no" while the Italians abstained. The Japanese contended that any changes had to be agreed upon unanimously, that they had a right to submit an alternate plan, and that the British forces had to leave by August 19.[63]

Peck tried to reach an understanding with his counterpart, Rear Admiral Moriji Takeda, commander of the Japanese naval landing party in Shanghai, but to no avail. Both sides asked for help through the diplomatic channels. From Hull, through Welles, Grew, and the consul in Shanghai, Richard P. Butrick, the State Department officials gave complete support to the military negotiators in Shanghai. Mr. Grew was informed in Tokyo on August 18 that if American troops tried to enter Sector B after the British departure they would be "opposed by Japanese forces."[64] Each side stiffened its resolve not to back down, yet not to challenge the other directly. The discussions in Shanghai developed into meetings between Rear Admiral Glassford, Commander, Yangtze Patrol, representing Admiral Hart, the Commander in Chief, Asiatic Fleet, and Vice Admiral Iwamura, representing Admiral Shigetaro Shimada, the Commander in Chief, China Sea Fleet. An interim arrangement, namely, to assign Sector B to the Shanghai Volunteer Corps until further agreement could be reached, became in actuality the existing arrangement until U.S. Marines were finally withdrawn from Shanghai to the Philippines during the first week in December 1941.

Just as the fall of France in June, with Italy's eleventh-hour entry to contribute to the coup de grace, upset the balance of power in Europe, threw American planners into a near-panic and compounded the turmoil in international relations in China, so did it affect the Japanese government. The pro-German elements, primarily in the army, were elated at the turn of events in Europe and, as might have been expected, the previously suppressed smouldering insistence on closer military ties with Germany flared into open flame. Moderates in the Yonai government and generally the Japanese admirals countered that Hitler could not easily overcome British sea power and that the end was not yet in sight. Despite the cautiousness on the part of the moderates and the admirals, the Army was determined not to let pass the golden opportunity to join with an obviously winning team. The war minister, General Shunroka Hata, was forced by the pro-Axis element of the army to resign on July 16 and, quite deliberately, there was no recommendation for a replacement. A new Cabinet was formed under Prince Fumimaro Konoye, who had been prime minister from 1937 to 1939. The new war minister was General Hideki Tojo. who was destined to become prime minister in October 1941 and take his country into war with the United States. Yosuka Matsuoka became the foreign minister ostensibly to counterbalance the influence of the army, but he was instrumental in Japan's joining the Axis in the Tripartite Pact within a few months. The fourth Cabinet member was Admiral Zengo Yoshida, the navy minister.

Meanwhile, Admiral Richardson finally had his trip to Washington, from July 7 to 11. After conferences with the CNO and the President, he conferred with Hornbeck, adviser on political relations in the State Department. He reaffirmed to each one what he had written and said many times before: that "neither the Navy nor the country was prepared for war with Japan" and if such an eventuality did happen it would be costly, drawn out, and with doubtful prospects of ultimate success. He returned to the fleet "with three distinct impressions":

> *First* That the Fleet was retained in the Hawaiian area solely to support diplomatic representations and as a deterrent to Japanese aggressive actions;
>
> *Second* That there was no intention of embarking on actual hostilities against Japan;
>
> *Third* That the immediate mission of the fleet was accelerated training and absorption of new personnel and the attainment of a

maximum condition of material and personnel readiness consistent with its retention in the Hawaiian area.[65]

Being out of the Washington mainstream, Richardson retained
these impressions through September when the newly appointed Secretary of the Navy, Colonel Frank Knox, visited him and the fleet. On
the request of Knox, Richardson prepared a long memorandum of
points which they had discussed. The main points Richardson drove
home during the Secretary's visit concerned the deficiencies of enlisted
men, both in numbers and training; the location of the fleet inhibit-
ing its ability to train and to prepare for war; his low appreciation of
"Navy Publicity;" and even worse opinion of cooperation between the
Executive, State, and War Departments with the Navy Department.
To emphasize his personal evaluation of the State Department's role
in the fleet's location, Richardson asked the rhetorical question:

> .... what is the State Department's conception of our next move?
> Does it believe that the Fleet is now mobilized and that it could em-
> bark on a campaign directly from Hawaii or safely conduct necessary
> training from the insecure anchorage of Lahaina which is 2000 miles
> nearer enemy submarine bases than our normal Pacific bases?[66]

Richardson's comments on navy publicity were a direct slap at
Stark's handling of the service party line in Washington. Richardson
had been assistant chief of naval operations under Admiral Leahy and
knew the Washington routine quite well. He was particularly concerned about those actions which were creating a "false sense of
security" in the United States: "... practically all Navy Publicity,
hearings before committees, speeches in Congress and handouts from
the Navy Department...."[67] It was Stark and his immediate subordinates in the Office of the Chief of Naval Operations, who were
responsible for navy publicity, who were doing the testifying before
committees in Congress and giving handouts from the department.
Richardson took a dim view of what he saw from the sidelines—that
too much emphasis was placed on the defensive nature of the Navy;
on the Navy as a "mobile Maginot Line behind which people can
reside in peace;" on the fleet being "fully manned, fully trained and
ready to fight at the drop of a hat;" on solely "material things" being
used as the basis for measuring comparative strengths of navies; and
on "aviation as a cheap means of defense." This type of publicity
statement he thought weakened "the moral fibre" of the country and
created an "unhealthy national morale in a country which may be
drawn into war on very short notice." The sincerity and alarm of the

Commander in Chief, United States Fleet, is best illustrated in his closing statement of that part of the memorandum:

> For a people, who may actually be involved in war in a comparatively short time, to be told that they can risk war without danger or wage war without risk, may be fatally detrimental to the determined prosecution of the very war towards which such conceptions inevitably lead.[68]

Nor did Richardson confine his critical comments to navy publicity. He did not consider that coordination and mutual understanding between the "Executive, State and War Departments with the Navy Department" was as close as was "necessary for effective action." He was responsible for the efficiency of the Navy "upon which the government relies to enforce National policy, when its aims cannot be secured by diplomatic means." To Richardson the existing policy appeared "to be headed towards forcing our will upon another Pacific Nation by diplomatic representations supported by economic measures, a large material Navy in process of construction, and the disposition of an inadequately manned *Fleet in being*." Then he asked if the country were prepared to face war or the inevitable loss of prestige if it were not. Had objectives of such a war been formulated and its costs considered and compared with the value of victory? He ended his long memorandum with observations on the Atlantic scene.

> Are objectives being formulated and plans made for our active participation in the European war? We cannot long remain half in and half out of such a war. We should decide now on definite objectives and plans and should not assume that we will fight this one like we did the last, i.e., by sending aviation and light forces for active participation and utilizing our heavy ships, in *secure* home bases, largely as training ships. Such a course would immobilize our heavy ships, which are most certainly going to be needed either in the Atlantic or the Pacific, depending on the progress of the war.[69]

Knox duly passed the Richardson memorandum to Stark in Washington.

A few days later Richardson wrote Stark that Knox, on his visit, had invited him to Washington in early October and that his reply at the time was that he could not go "to Washington except under orders, but if Stark wanted to see" him, he supposed he would be ordered. He told Stark that he did not know "any benefit to the Navy that would accrue" from his coming to Washington, since he "had fully and frankly expressed his views to the Secretary on all points where he felt such expression might help the Navy or the Nation."

(Since Stark had Richardon's memorandum to Secretary Knox, he probably could not have agreed more with this statement.) In a postscript to a short letter he reiterated once again that he had "nothing to take up with the Department that cannot be handled by correspondence," but that if he were wanted in Washington he was ready to come upon his arrival in San Pedro the last part of September.[70]

Between Richardson's trip to Washington in July and Knox's visit to Hawaii in September a laboriously conceived and unprecedented maneuver finally came to the execution phase. On September 3, 1940, the United States transferred fifty World War I type destroyers and other war materials to Britain in exchange for two bases and ninety-nine-year leases on other potential base sites, all in British possessions in the western Atlantic. In the latter part of September events moved faster and faster. On September 22, Japan extracted from Vichy France an agreement for the use of three airfields, the stationing of troops, and the rights of passage in northern Indochina. On September 24, after spirited discussion between the President, his military and cabinet advisers over a total embargo of goods to Japan (Stark and Welles were definitely against further embargo of oil), all iron and steel scrap shipments to Japan were officially stopped. The next day a new loan to China was announced. Although negotiations had been under way for weeks, the signing in Berlin on September 27 of the Tripartite Pact, a defense alliance binding Germany, Italy, and Japan together, appeared to be an answer to U.S. actions protesting Japanese moves in northern Indochina.

The Joint Planning Committee was pessimistic in a report to Stark and Marshall on the day of the Tripartite signing. They saw no assurance that Japan would not, within the next few months, move swiftly either against the Dutch East Indies or against the Philippines or Guam, especially if the Japanese government should become increasingly embarrassed by embargoes on exports in the Far East, and should at the same time become convinced that, despite United States statements, it was bluffing and would back down in the face of serious challenge. If the situation in the Far East deteriorated to the point that armed opposition to Japan became necessary, even in the face of the potential threat in the Atlantic, the planners recommended that the action be limited "to minor naval surface and air forces operating from Singapore and Dutch East Indies bases, plus the interruption of Japanese shipping in the eastern Pacific."[71]

The Japanese actions in Indochina, their obduracy over the Defense Sector problems in Shanghai, and a generally increased belligerency prompted Admiral Hart to write Stark that "the situation seems to be rapidly changing as regards the relative importance of this command's two missions." Hart's peacetime mission of guarding American lives and interests was being overtaken by the "necessity of being 'set' in the other part of our job out here." Since the *Augusta* was so vulnerable in Shanghai and since he considered Admiral Glassford and Colonel Peck well qualified to take care of any situation on the Yangtze or in Shanghai, he planned to move his ships to Manila. At Hart's suggestion, which was readily endorsed by Ambassador Grew in Japan and the Navy Department, Secretary Hull issued a directive to his diplomatic and consular officers in China, Japan, Hong Kong, and Indochina to suggest to all American citizens in their areas that they evacuate. Through October 1940, most of the women and children and many of the businessmen and missionaries did so, in the passenger ships *Monterey* and *Mariposa* of the Matson Lines and the *Washington* of the United States Lines. Still, Hart was concerned "about leaving too many 'hostages to fortune'—in the shape of Marines and river gunboat personnel in China."[72] The getting-set phase had started—and well over a year before hostilities commenced.

On the other side of the world, decisions were being made affecting the Japanese in China. It appeared in October that Britain had weathered the threat of invasion by Germany without any further aggression by Japan against British strongholds in the Pacific. On October 4, immediately after the British Cabinet had decided to reopen the Burma Road on October 17, Churchill sent a message to Roosevelt urging him to send a sizable naval detachment to Singapore— "the bigger the better," as a display of the English-speaking naval power arrayed against Japan. Stark, Marshall, and Welles were vehemently against such a move, while Secretary Stimson urged shifting the bulk of the fleet to Singapore forthwith. Stark observed, in the meeting of the Standing Liaison Committee when the Churchill proposal was discussed, that "every day that we are able to maintain peace and still support the British is valuable time gained," while Marshall stated that "this was as unfavorable a moment as you could choose" for inviting trouble.[73] At the very time of the British proposal for an American show of force in Singapore, the admirals in the United States Navy were united in urging that the fleet be brought back to San Diego and San Pedro. The State Department, particularly Dr. Hornbeck, considered the fleet a deterrent to Japan and withdrawal after the Tripartite Pact signing would possibly indicate fear of the new Axis Union.

Admiral Richardson was summoned to Washington to participate in the discussions of the future employment of the fleet. He was most upset to find out from Knox and Stark, prior to speaking with Roosevelt, that instead of bringing the fleet to the West Coast, there was serious talk of reinforcing the Asiatic Fleet and of sending the Singapore detachment requested by the British government. On October 8, Richardson and Leahy had lunch with Roosevelt, who inquired whether sending reinforcements to the Asiatic Fleet would serve to deter Japan. Leahy thought it might have a temporary effect, but since the Asiatic Fleet might well be lost, only the least valuable combatant ships should be sent. Roosevelt did not mention sending a detachment to Singapore, but what he did suggest dismayed Richardson so much that he later asked Knox if the President was considering declaring war on Japan. If Japan was to take "drastic action" in retaliation for the reopening of the Burma Road, Roosevelt had told Knox, he was thinking of a complete embargo and the establishment of a naval patrol in two lines, one from Hawaii west to the Philippines and the other between Samoa and the Netherlands East Indies.

Suddenly this newest insight into Roosevelt's thinking meshed with the points he had covered the day before. On October 9, Richardson was told to go ahead assembling the train—support and supply vessels—for the fleet, was asked if there were enough fuel oil in Samoa for four old light cruisers, was told that a division of such ships might be sent to Mindanao in the Philippines as a gesture, and was asked for a chart showing British and French bases or possible bases for surface ships, submarines, or airplanes in the Pacific islands east of the International Date Line. Roosevelt also discussed Ghormley's liaison with the Admiralty and British desire for staff conferences. Lastly, Richardson recorded Roosevelt as having said:

> I can be convinced of the desirability of retaining the battleships on the West Coast if I can be given a good statement which will convince the American people, and the Japanese Government, that in bringing the battleships to the West Coast we are not stepping backward.[74]

Richardson tried to reason with Knox over the consequences of establishing the two lines of patrol. The fleet was not ready for such patrols, much less for war, and surely, if Japanese commerce were intercepted, war was inevitable. Knox was more sympathetic to Stimson's and Roosevelt's hard-line approaches than to excuses of unreadiness. He told Richardson on October 10 that if he did not like Roosevelt's plans, then he and Stark could draw up their own to accomplish the same purpose.[75] Richardson, the realist, did just that. With his own War Plans Officer and the officers in the War Plans Division of Stark's staff, he drew up a list of assumptions, paralleling those of Roosevelt's, of retaliatory actions by Japan against Britain should the Burma Road be reopened. A skeleton operations plan was also written redistributing forces throughout the Pacific—including the provision for a comparatively strong detachment of four cruisers, a carrier, nine destroyers, four minesweepers, and two auxiliaries—for possible dispatch to the Netherlands East Indies to be under the operational control of Commander in Chief, Asiatic Fleet. Richardson left his plan with Stark for review and submission to the Secretary of the Navy and the President.

By coincidence, while Richardson was in Washington discussing the future employment of the fleet, Secretary Knox presented Roosevelt with a long list of recommended actions necessary to prepare for war. The recommendations were not limited to those for which the Navy alone was responsible or to preparation for preparation's sake, but additionally included acts to impress the Japanese government. The memorandum showed his propensity for recommending cross-departmental actions:

> Orders have been issued for these measures to be taken at once:
> 1. Call the organized Naval and Marine Reserves.
> 2. Call Fleet Reserves, Navy and Marine, selective basis.
> 3. Lay nets and booms for drill purposes.

> The following steps in preparation for war can be taken to impress the Japanese with the seriousness of our preparations:
> 1. Army send reinforcement to Hawaii if contemplated.
> 2. Presidential proclamation for Maritime Commission to requisition merchant ships, in order to
> 3. Take over tankers, transports, auxiliaries, and begin to assemble Train on W. Coast.
> 4. Coast Guard transfer to Navy.
> 5. Fill up garrisons of defense battalions in 14th District outlying bases.
> 6. Presidential proclamation establishing defensive sea areas.
> 7. Withdraw nationals from China. (Inconsistent with getting merchant ships out of danger.)
> 8. Plan for evacuation of families out of Hawaii and later Panama.
> 9. Preparations regarding seizure German and Japanese merchant vessels in ports and near our coasts.
> 10. Pressure on Britain to speed leases Bermuda and Newfoundland (essential).

11. Change laws to take limit off naval and marine personnel—limit to President's discretion.
12. Prepare plans for concentration camps (Army—Justice).
13. Executive Order to call Volunteer Reserves, including communications and merchant marine reserves.
14. Withdraw Marines from North China (this means Embassy should be closed). Leave very small token force. Stop sending replacements, Marine Shanghai—let attrition operate. Consider withdrawal when currency situation permits.
15. Netherlands East Indies:—Assist in material; line up for mutual support.

The following are matters for Treasury and State:
1. Freeze credits and assets of Japan.
2. Continue to bolster Chinese credit.
3. Take such steps as may be necessary to insure Chinese currency carrying on in case Shanghai is occupied by Japan.

For consideration, but in abeyance for the moment:
1. Alert the Asiatic Station at once to get ships other than gunboats out of China. This should be the first secret step.
2. Alert the: Naval Establishment (Established security patrols, etc.)
   Military Establishment
   Merchant Marine (Clippers)
   Department of Justice—sabotage—surveillance of agents
   Panama Canal—all security measures.[76]

Roosevelt's answer the next day was short and to the point. It was the answer of a commander in chief up for reelection who could not be as aggressive as his service secretaries proposed.

In relations to Secret Memorandum of October ninth, covering measures to be taken in preparation for war, I approve the first three. Please do not put any of the others into effect without speaking to me about them. F.D.R.[77]

Upon his return to the West Coast Richardson wrote to Hart giving him the history of the Washington visit and the evolution of his substitute plan, after citing the "impracticability" of the original Roosevelt concept of the two patrol lines. Richardson pointed out that his plan was similar to the old *Orange Plan* except that the fleet was restricted from going any further than mid-Pacific because of the Atlantic situation, that there would be no Army units involved, and that the United States Fleet would have the use of the facilities at Singapore. In the event that the assumptions were not realized prior to January 1, 1941, or the decision had not been made prior to that time to send the advanced detachment to the Asiatic Fleet, a train would be assembled and a full scale exercise would be made against Christmas Island, near the equator due south of Hawaii. Coincidental with the exercise the Asiatic Fleet would be reinforced so that Japan would realize the United States' determination and capability to protect its national interests.[78] At the time of his October 16 letter to Hart, Richardson had not heard from Washington of the status of his plan, nor would he hear. Roosevelt, and his more aggressive advisers, were apparently satisfied with other contemporary actions. The Army had decided to send two squadrons of pursuit airplanes to the Philippines, and the Navy planned to base ten additional submarines for the Asiatic Fleet in Manila Bay, Australia had agreed to make fifty additional planes available for the defense of Singapore.[79]

Richardson waited a few more days after writing to Hart and, having received no further information, sent Stark a long analysis of "War Plans-Status and readiness of in view of the current international situation." He set the tenor of the seriousness of his letter in the first paragraph. He felt that it was

> ...his solemn duty to present, for the Chief of Naval Operations, certain facts and conclusions in order that there may be no doubt in the minds of higher authority as to his convictions in regard to the present situation especially in the Pacific.[80]

He reviewed the differences he found in the thinking in Washington between his July and October trips, after which he analyzed the *Orange Plan* and its supporting United States Fleet War Plans. None of them were current or realistic in the present international situation. Next he reviewed the *Rainbow* series plans. The only two plans he had, *Rainbows 1* and *2*, were inapplicable; the former pertained only to the Western Hemisphere and the latter, which Richardson had in draft form only, concerned sustaining the democratic powers in the Pacific. According to Richardson there existed a vital necessity for a new directive, possibly *Rainbow 3*, "based on present realities, national objectives and commitments as far as these are known or can be predicted at the present time," and there should be "coordination of plans developed with National Policy and steps to be taken to implement that policy." He had no intention or desire "to evade his legitimate responsibilities" nor was anything in his letter to be so construed. He realized fully that "no plan can foresee or provide for every possible situation, and that adjustments and re-estimates must be made to fit the actual situation presented." Yet, at the same time, he "most strongly believed" that he "must be better informed than he [had been] as to the Department's plans and intentions if he [was] to perform his full duty."[81]

Richardson would not receive a *Rainbow 3* plan or an answer to his complaints about not being sufficiently informed until the latter part of December, almost two months later. When he did hear from Stark again, it was after Roosevelt's reelection. On November 12, Stark wrote to both Richardson and Hart about the genesis of his detailed analysis of future courses of action. At that time his "broad estimate" was in Roosevelt's hands. Both fleet commanders would have to wait for details of the yet-to-be-identified *Plan Dog*. In the meantime, Stark promised both a *Rainbow 3* plan "in a few days," even though the Army war planners had stopped work on *Rainbows 2* and *3* on May 23. Stark reaffirmed to Richardson his certainty that the United States would enter the war. He wrote:

> ... you know I have felt right along that it is only a matter of time before we get in [though I can not say this out loud]. The chief question that concerns us is *where* we get in, and *whom* we will fight—and "tomorrow" or perhaps "today" is what I am working towards.
>
> You have received the despatch directing the sending of submarines to Manila. There are no plans at present to send anything more in that direction. But present conditions are far from static, the Japanese appear to be making preparation for a definite move of some kind, and the answer we will give, if any, to the steps they may take in the future can not be predicted at this time.[82]

To Hart's letter Stark added the importance of "laying, with the British and possibly the Dutch, a framework for a future plan of co-operation, should we be forced into the war." This followed the words of caution which were to be the stumbling block to anything constructive in discussions on the Far East through the next year: "The Navy can, of course, make no political commitments. Therefore we can make no specific military plans for an allied war."[83]

Nevertheless, discussions with the British were the order of the day. Hull had favored, and advocated to Lord Lothian, "technical talks" between the military leaders of the United States and Britain. Roosevelt had a special observer in Rear Admiral Ghormley for liaison with the Admiralty, which, with Churchill, had been pushing hard for closer cooperation, especially in the Far East. Rejection of the proposal for the United States to send a strong detachment to Singapore did not dampen the British drive for "staff conversations." Rumors in October of important conversations to be held in Washington concerning the Far East were first confirmed by the White House, as a warning to Japan, then, for political reasons, denied because Roosevelt was being accused in the campaign of making secret commitments to Britain. Ghormley was instructed to exchange information but to make no commitments, implied or otherwise, concerning possible United States participation in the Far East.

After the election, new impetus for conversations came from two different directions. Lord Lothian, upon his return from London, saw Hull on November 25 and again raised the question "of conferences between the naval experts of [the] two Governments with respect to what each would or might do in case of military outbreaks on the part of Japan."[84] Additionally, Stark's *Plan Dog*, which had not been accepted yet by the President, War or State Departments, ended with the paragraph:

> Accordingly, I make the recommendation that, as a preliminary to possible entry of the United States into the conflict, the United States Army and Navy at once undertake secret staff talks on technical matters with the British military and naval authorities in London, with Canadian military authorities in Washington, and with British and Dutch authorities in Singapore and Batavia. The purpose would be to reach agreements and lay down plans for promoting unity of allied effort should the United States find it necessary to enter the war under any of the alternative eventualities considered in this memorandum.*

With presidential approval, Stark sent a personal invitation to Admiral of the Fleet Sir Dudley Pound on November 30 to send accredited representatives to Washington before Christmas if possible. The exchange of preliminary information and the development of position papers by each side delayed the meeting until January 1941. The basis of the American position in January would be Stark's *Plan Dog*.

Late in November, Stark asked Richardson for a more detailed analysis of defense requirements for the protection of the fleet in Pearl Harbor. The last two replies received to similar inquiries made to Admiral Bloch, Commandant, Fourteenth Naval District, were "not very definite" and Stark needed more ammunition to get the War Department to put more effort into the buildup of defense against carrier air attack. Stark admitted that the highly successful British carrier raid on November 11 against the Italian fleet anchored at Taranto prompted his concern for the safety of the fleet at Pearl Harbor. That

* For *Plan Dog* see Appendix A.

concern had "to do both with possible activities on the part of Japanese residents of Hawaii and with the possibilities of attack coming from overseas. By far the most profitable object of sudden attack in Hawaiian waters would be the Fleet units based in that area."[85] Richardson's preliminary answer, written before he returned to Pearl Harbor from the West Coast, was that torpedo nets, proposed by Stark, within the harbor were neither necessary nor practicable, that he would take up the matter of protection with Admiral Bloch, and that he would issue a plan for tighter security measures when he arrived at Pearl Harbor.

In mid-December Richardson received, by officer messenger from Stark, four advanced copies of *Navy Basic War Plan—Rainbow No. 3.* By a letter of December 17, Stark defended both *Rainbow 3* and his past cooperation with Richardson. *Rainbow 3* was "designed to provide against the most imminent and difficult war situation which may confront the United States in the near future... where the principal portion of the national effort is directed westward." Richardson's task relative to the new plan was quite clear:

> It is, therefore requested that the Commander in Chief prepare as soon as practicable the operating plans for a war envisaged by *Rainbow No. 3.*[86]

Stark did mention that there were "under study... by the naval and army officials... plans based on assumptions requiring the exertion of the principal portion of the national effort to the eastward (*Rainbow No. 5*) and also a plan, somewhat similar to *Rainbow No. 1*, involving the defense of the entire Western Hemisphere against attack from both the east and the west (*Rainbow No. 4*)." He considered the three plans "adequate to guide mobilization, initial deployment, and initial operations under all contingencies which [were] foreseeable."

He then chided Richardson a bit about the *Orange Plan*. He believed it was unnecessary to comment upon the applicability of the *Orange Plan*, "as that Plan was drawn up to guide the prosecution of a war under circumstances which do not now exist." He asserted that he had kept the fleet commander in chief "advised as to all matters within his own knowledge which related to current national policy and pending national decisions," and that his past practice would be continued in the future. Richardson was reminded that "the changing world military situation will continue to affect policy, and thus will influence plans for the war operation of the naval forces." It was "impracticable to draw up and to issue new Navy Basic War Plans when merely minor changes in policy occur." A few days later Stark wrote a long letter in which he discussed the assembly of a train for the fleet and the exercise at Christmas Island which Richardson had proposed to Hart. He ended that letter on his by then usual ominous note:

> There is little that I can add which is not repetition, but I shall repeat just the same that every 24 hours past is just one day nearer to actual hostilities and that your flag officers and captains should be completely in the frame of mind that we will be in the fighting business most any time, and purely as a guess on my own part, I would say at any time after the next 90 days. Our heads and our hearts and every ounce of energy that we have should be devoted exclusively to the business of war and keeping fit—and I don't mean maybe.
>
> It may come anytime.[87]

In neither letter did Stark mention his *Plan Dog* to which he had referred in passing in his November 12 letter. *Rainbow 3* was Richardson's guidance.

As 1940 drew to a close, the situation since the previous January had changed considerably. Stark, who had forecast something breaking quickly and without warning in the Far East in January, did not know in December where the United States would commence fighting but predicted that it would be fighting soon. His attention, nevertheless, was concentrated on helping Britain in the Atlantic. In China, the United States Navy's confrontations with the Imperial Japanese Navy had been less acrimonious and less frequent than in previous years. As the year ended with Hart "getting set" for other contingencies, with the British and the French military forces, the American dependents and American combatant ships withdrawn, relations were quiescent. To be sure, the whole Far East was not so. Japanese forces, jockeying for position in Indochina, posed new threats to Singapore and the Netherlands East Indies and reinforced the fears of future aggression by having formally joined the Tripartite Pact. The United States explored ways to cooperate with China, Britain, and the Netherlands to counteract the Japanese moves; the noose of economic sanctions, having been finally fashioned, was drawing slowly but fatally around Japan.

Richardson, who had balked at his fleet being held at Pearl Harbor for the politically reasoned deterrent effect, had lost each of his persuasive attempts to get it to the West Coast bases so that he might better prepare it for the inevitable war. The year ended with him preparing war plans for actions in the western Pacific based on a hastily completed *Rainbow 3* plan which would be cancelled in just eight more months.

In Washington, alarm at the highly successful German blitzkrieg had triggered multiple decisions. American aid to Britain had increased in volume and acceptability after the first threats of invasion had passed. Mid-year also saw the start of the two-ocean navy, the swearing in of two new aggressive service secretaries, Knox and Stimson, and a decision by Roosevelt to run for a third term.

The year ended with the stage set for discussions in Washington and the Far East with the British and possibly Dutch military leaders to cooperate more closely in the Atlantic and the Pacific against potentially common enemies. The incentive for talks in both areas was from the Chief of Naval Operations and the basis for the United States position would be of naval origin.

CHAPTER 6

Japan's Growing Need
For Petroleum

It is highly probable that the aircraft which attacked Pearl Harbor
and the carriers which transported them across the Pacific operated on
American fuel.[1]

Two of the major prerequisites to any war machine are steel and
petroleum and for both commodities Japan, since its modernization,
depended heavily upon imports. Approximately 80 percent of Japan's
crude oil and refined stocks in the early 1930s was imported from the
United States, and from those imports Japan had accumulated a reserve for war. The war machine put into motion against China in
1937 required vast amounts of aviation gasoline and lubricants, fuel
oil for ships, gasoline for land vehicles, and the various forms of oil
used in the civilian economy to support the war. Yet by 1939 the carefully nurtured reserve had grown to a maximum of fifty-five million
barrels.[2] If all oil imports were cut off, the reserve would last less than
two years at the 1939 rate of consumption. However, the unexpected
tempo of the war in China and the failure to bring that war to an
early end threatened to cut into the precious reserve. Only an increased volume of imports would allow the reserve to be maintained,
and, of course, to build it up despite the increased usage required an
even larger volume of imports.

Reports of startling Japanese demands for accelerated imports
reached the State Department in June and July 1940. The recent fall
of France and the Battle of Britain were very much the major topics
of concern in Washington. Did the increased demands for oil portend
a Japanese move to the south or were they part of a build-up of a
larger reserve for a long war in the Pacific?

Before Secretary Hull departed for a conference in Havana on

92

July 19, he rejected suggestions that he advocate to the President cutting oil exports to Japan to their normal volume.[3] Mr. Hull probably remembered Ambassador Grew's words of warning to President Roosevelt the year before "that if we cut off Japanese supplies of oil and that if Japan then finds that she cannot obtain sufficient oil from other commercial sources to ensure national security, she will in all probability send her fleet down to take the Dutch East Indies."[4]

On the day Hull left for Havana, Roosevelt conferred with Stimson, Knox, and Welles on a proposal passed to him by Secretary of the Treasury Henry Morgenthau, Jr. The proposal had been suggested in part by Lord Lothian, the British ambassador, who had discussed the matter with Stimson, Knox, Morgenthau, and the Australian minister, Richard Casey, at a dinner party the previous evening. The plan proposed by Lothian was for the United States, on the grounds of national defense, to stop all exports of oil. Britain would then get all its oil from the Caribbean area, arranging with the Dutch government in the meantime to destroy the oil wells in the Indies. Finally, the British would concentrate bombing attacks on the synthetic oil plants in Germany. "Where then, and how, would Japan and Germany get oil for war?"[5] Welles objected to the Morgenthau endorsement of the Lothian proposal and to embargoes against Japan in general because he believed that they would cause Japan to make war on Britain.

As a result of the July 19 meeting, Welles entered into a series of consultations with the President and Admiral Stark. A ban on oil might force the Japanese to make a decision about going into the Dutch East Indies and Welles doubted that the American people were ready to support a counter military move. He thought he had impressed Roosevelt with his argument,[6] and from later evidence he most probably had the support of Stark in his persuasive efforts.

Some cabinet members were much more prone to take a firm stand against Japan. The "hard line element" of Morgenthau, Stimson, and Knox actually succeeded in getting the President to sign a proclamation on July 25, 1940, to establish export controls over all kinds of oil and scrap metals. Welles and his worried state department subordinates were disturbed on learning of that move, because they feared that the embargo would "provoke a crisis with Japan sooner or later, and probably sooner." Welles argued his case again and managed to persuade Roosevelt to issue a State Department version of a control proclamation "to make clear the proclamation of July 25." That version applied export controls only to "aviation motor fuels and lubricants and No. 1 heavy melting iron and steel scrap."[7] The export controls desired by the hard-liners were thereby emasculated. Not until a year later were the strict controls to be evoked.

The term "aviation motor fuel" was further defined in the Presidential Proclamation of July 26, 1940 as "High octane gasolines, hydrocarbons, and hydrocarbon mixtures which, with the addition of tetraethyl lead up to a total content of 3 c.c. per gallon will exceed 87 octane number, or any material from which by commercial distillation there can be separated more than 3 per cent of such gasoline, hydrocarbon, or hydrocarbon mixture."[8] The question of circumventing the restriction on petroleum exports based on octane level became the center of controversy between those who viewed the proclamation as the minimum move in the right direction toward "tight" control and those who viewed the proclamation as a guide to maximum limits of control against Japan.

Many naval officers wanted the export controls rigidly enforced by applying restrictions to *all* fuels which could be made to serve as aviation fuel through the use of additives with or without further distillation. The section of the Navy Department best informed on efforts to circumvent the octane limits and most anxious to restrict the Japanese efforts to increase their reserve was the Office of Naval Intelligence.

The Director of Naval Intelligence, Rear Admiral Walter Stratton Anderson, informed the Chief of Naval Operations that through reliable sources his agents had information "regarding negotiations being carried on between the Associated Oil Company, Standard Oil Company of California and Japanese oil interests which appeared to be aimed at circumventing the export on aviation gasoline." Japanese importers were able "to obtain not only Kettleman fuel oil [a partially refined oil] but a special blend of crude from Kettleman rated at 89 octane." The American oil companies concerned were near agreement with the Japanese interests "to supply this special 89 octane crude against outstanding large orders for 97 octane, 92 hi-octane and 87 octane fuel." By suitable leading of this special blend with ethyl, practically all Japanese requirements for high octane fuel could be met regardless of export control. Whether or not this "special blend" was a commercial grade, or a blend developed for the purpose of satisfying Japanese requirements, was not known to the intelligence agents at that time.[9] It was highly significant to them, however, that by using a special blend of *crude* oil, which was not restricted, the Japanese could meet their gasoline needs. Since ship bunker fuel was not restricted, Japan could meet all its petroleum requirements.

Records do not indicate what, if anything, Admiral Stark did or thought about the specific information on circumvention, but four days later the Director of Naval Intelligence wrote directly to the Secretary of the Navy with *a carbon copy to the Chief of Naval Operations and the naval aide to the President.* After reviewing the circumvention techniques being worked out by certain American oil companies with the Japanese, Admiral Anderson pointed out how the desired degree of embargo against Japan could be made air-tight and such schemes of circumvention be defeated. First, it was necessary for the proper governmental authorities, presumably the State and Treasury Departments, to set forth exactly what degree of embargo they desired to enforce. Then, qualified commercial oil experts could assist in the implementation of that policy by writing the necessary rules with the proper technical specifications to make the policy really binding. Admiral Anderson added that while the navy was not charged with the primary responsibility in connection with the enforcement of any embargo, such an embargo was definitely of Navy interest, and "it is believed the Departments charged with enforcing the embargo would welcome suggestions from the Navy in the premises."[10]

The memorandum from Admiral Anderson was dually significant. First, it stated a position for the Navy, namely, that the embargo of oil was of interest to the Navy, which was ready to give suggestions on how better to enforce that embargo. The feeling expressed by the Director of Naval Intelligence was not shared by the Chief of Naval Operations which probably accounts for the direct correspondence with the Secretary. It was quite "legal" for Admiral Anderson so to correspond, but it was not the accepted procedure. The second significance of the memorandum concerns its treatment after Secretary Knox received it. Not only was Knox in agreement with the suggestions contained in the subject memorandum, he wanted to share them with the leader of the "hard line" group, Secretary Morgenthau. On Admiral Anderson's memorandum he pencilled a note to James Forrestal, then under secretary of the navy, telling him to "take this up with Henry Morgenthau early next week" and to "ask Admiral Anderson for a copy of [the] letter he has on this subject and give that to H.M. also."[11] Obviously, part of the navy favored tight controls.

One of the first indications of the feelings of the Chief of Naval Operations on the subject of embargo of oil to Japan was contained in a letter of September 24, 1940, to Admiral Richardson, Commander in Chief, United States Fleet. The previous day, Stark had spent over three hours in the State Department, of which two hours were spent in the morning with Hull, Welles, and Hornbeck and an hour in the afternoon with Welles alone. In those meetings Stark strongly opposed an embargo on fuel oil to Japan. He left feeling that Welles was "in complete agreement" with him and that Hull had raised the issue to have a thorough discussion on the subject.[12] Stark was in the camp of Welles and certainly not that of Morgenthau.

If Stark did not like the look of things on September 24, he would like them less three days later. On September 27, the Tripartite Pact between Japan, Germany, and Italy was signed, increasing the chance that the United States would eventually fight Japan. A clash was possible if the United States—in support of Britain against her opponent, Germany—encountered the Japanese in support of Germany against Britain. Fear that the new formal alliance was a prelude to a Japanese move against Singapore or the East Indies prompted many discussions in Washington. Within the State Department, one faction, including Hornbeck, stood for further use at once of American economic power as a deterrent, while Hamilton and his associates in the Far Eastern Division advised otherwise—unless the United States was prepared for war. Morgenthau, Stimson and Secretary of the Interior, Harold L. Ickes, who was also petroleum administrator for national defense, wanted to lower the octane levels of exports, and in the Navy, though Knox still seemed inclined to use pressure, "the admirals from Stark down were saying the Navy was not ready for war."[13]

Meanwhile the Dutch were asking the State Department to refrain from actions which would increase Japanese pressure against the Indies. Stimson's suggestion of sending a flying squadron of warships to the Indies to deter Japanese actions was strongly opposed by Admirals Stark and Richardson. Stark and General Marshall recognized that a conflict with Japan in the near future was altogether probable, but they insisted that the United States was as yet unprepared for hostilities in the Pacific and that, in any event, it was more in the American interests to arm against Hitler and support Britain than to devote a major effort against Japan.[14]

A naval intelligence report on November 2 showed that, despite the licensing of exports since July, aviation gasoline shipments to Japan jumped to a new height two months later. Department of Commerce figures[15] for exports to Japan read:

| | *Barrels* | |
	Aviation Gas	Other Gas
July	40,938	119,277
August	8,540	283,550
September	115,051	434,284

When the intelligence agents questioned the Division of Controls (State Department) about the big increase they were informed that while the figures were accurate they were based "upon the presumption that any gasoline suitable for use or actually used in aeroplanes is *aviation gasoline*" and that the controls office used a stricter definition in terms of octane count. Officials there did admit that a very large proportion of the gasoline exported to Japan was actually used in planes and was stepped up by "boosters" to high octane count. Personnel in the Division of Controls also stated that the question was essentially political insofar as they were under instructions to follow "a lenient policy designed to appease Japan and relieve the Netherlands East Indies of pressure."[16]

Under the circumstances the State Department had little choice. The Navy was reluctant to deploy forces to the Far East and was not ready to fight Japan. Tight restrictions might force Japan to take the alternate source of supply. Lenient policy might buy time to prepare for war. It was against this background that Admiral Stark evolved his *Plan Dog,* which proposed American military support of Britain to defeat Germany and if forced to fight in the Pacific against Japan, to fight a defensive war using economic restrictions to limit the Japanese. Economic measures were to be used in a war, not to start one. Stark looked upon the embargo of oil to Japan as an unnecessary risk of war—he wanted no war until Germany was defeated.

While Stark was working out his *Plan Dog* memorandum, the British were active in attempting to get the cooperation of the United States against Japan. Lord Lothian on November 1 asked the American government to join Britain in limiting the total exports of all essential goods to Japan to only "normal" amounts."[17] Later in the month the question of restricting oil exports boiled up again. On November 20, the British sent Admiral Stark a long memorandum entitled *Japanese Oil Situation,* which reviewed in detail their intelligence on the matter. The key to the figures in the papers relative to the reserve of Japanese oil were based on the United States Navy's estimate of consumption for the last three years. The British were of the opinion, based on their war experience, that the estimate of consumption was too high and that in fact the Japanese were not as hard-pressed for oil as the U.S. Navy thought. They further proposed "that the only reliable means of dealing with the very undesirable situation inherent in further accumulation of stocks by the Japanese would be by joint policy designed to curtail Japanese chartering of foreign flag tankers." Their policy was not to cut Japan off from supplies but to cooperate with the U.S. government in restricting, by the least provocative means, Japanese imports of oil from continuing at a rate for which there was no commercial justification.[18]

The offer had merit but Hull insisted that any action which might provoke the Japanese was unwise unless the British and American forces in the Far East were stronger. Stark, who wanted to concentrate on winning the Atlantic war first, was undoubtedly influenced by Richardson's constant plea for more trained personnel and support ships. Richardson considered the fleet, in its existing state of readiness, to be unprepared for war. In Washington he had argued as strongly as he could for returning it to the West Coast, where it could prepare for war and be provided an adequate train of support. Hull and Admiral Stark, to whom the British proposals were primarily directed, let them rest. Stark had already proposed joint discussions with the British to arrive at a better basis of possible future operations together.

Although the British government "accepted the decision" of Hull and Stark,[19] there was another attempt to get consideration on their memorandum, *Japanese Oil Situation*. A copy of the paper was given to Rear Admiral Ghormley, the special naval observer in London, who forwarded it to the Chief of Naval Operations. In his forwarding letter Ghormley asked his chief to note that the proposals "contained herein were presented to the State Department on November 20th, 1940, but no reply from State Department has yet been received." Ghormley suggested to Stark that in view of conditions in the Far East the British proposals "be given careful consideration as a possible deterrent to Japan becoming engaged in war at this time."[20] Ghormley did not know, of course, that the proposals had been carefully considered by Hull and Stark and shelved.

Discussions within the Cabinet and the State Department through the following months concentrated on freezing Japan's American assets and placing further restrictions on oil. In the meantime, Japanese imports of gasoline and crude oils from which aviation gasoline could be obtained continued to increase. State Department estimates in April 1941 were that the Japanese would receive from the United States and the Dutch East Indies over twelve million barrels during that year or three times the normal amount.

Despite Admiral Stark's feeling on the embargo of oil, Japanese practices in the procurement of oil on the West Coast could not continue without comment by the Navy to the State Department. In accordance with recognized international procedures the Japanese government obtained from the State Department permission for each

Japanese naval ship to visit United States ports. The State Department personnel always advised the Navy Department and requested comment. In April Secretary Knox informed Hull that the Navy Department had no objection to a proposed Japanese ship visit, but called attention to the recent frequency of Japanese naval visits. A total of twelve Japanese naval vessels had obtained cargoes of oil from the United States within a period of six months, five of those within sixty days. Certain of the vessels listed as naval vessels had made previous similar trips in their original status as commercial vessels. It appeared more than probable that their naval status had been devised to bestow upon them, and upon their obvious purposes, a degree of immunity which commercial vessels could scarcely command. Secretary Knox suggested that the frequency of such visits was "to say the least, unusual" and "that some restrictive policy would be a timely precaution to prevent the abuse of international courtesy."[21]

The fact that the frequency of the visits had increased to one every ten days[22] through February and March was disturbing enough, but the abuse of designating commercial vessels as naval vessels was more than the naval intelligence division cared to tolerate. The courtesies of the port allowed too much freedom to the crew for the many facets of espionage work, and to accord commercial vessels the honors due to men-of-war was highly unpalatable. On the recommendation of the Director of Naval Intelligence, Secretary Knox informed Secretary Hull on May 23 that oil cargo ships posing as Japanese men-of-war need not be accorded "the privileges, immunities and courtesies which would be accorded with pleasure to any recognized ship of the Japanese Navy." The case in point was the *Kokuyo Maru* which had last visited San Francisco in a commercial status and now requested the courtesy given a man-of-war on a proposed visit to Los Angeles. What really incensed the Navy was that, in answer to the question of the commanding officer's identity, the Japanese had replied that the senior officer aboard was a naval inspector with no indication that the ship was under his command. Under these circumstances the State Department was told that the *Kokuyo Maru* could enter Los Angeles as a commercial vessel, but if the Japanese insisted on the courtesies of a "bona-fide man-of-war, the Navy Department does not consider such requests as legitimate and recommends that in this case, and all subsequent similar cases, the Japanese Government be informed that the visit is not convenient."[23]

The Navy would not have to concern itself about Japanese naval tankers for many more months. On June 20, 1941, due to an actual domestic scarcity on the East Coast and as a move against the Axis powers, oil exports from the East Coast were restricted to the British Empire, the British forces in Egypt, and the Western Hemisphere. Arguments among cabinet members over restricting oil exports from both coasts resulted in Secretary Ickes threatening to resign. Stark and Welles had again delayed cutting off oil to Japan. In July the tempo quickened. Japan was poised to acquire additional bases in Indochina. On Roosevelt's direction, Acting Secretary of State Welles informed British Ambassador Halifax that "if Japan now took any overt step through force or through the exercise of pressure to conquer or to acquire alien territories in the Far East, the Government of the United States would immediately impose various embargoes, both economic and financial."[24] The showdown on the embargo question grew near.

Among those with whom Roosevelt conferred on the oil embargo was Admiral Stark. Stark described his feelings to Welles in a letter afterwards. In mid-July Roosevelt had asked Stark for his reaction to an embargo on a number of commodities to Japan, and was given the same answer as before, but in addition, Stark said he would have the War Plans Division make "a quick study." The study was finished on July 21 and sent to the President. A copy was also sent to Hull, and Stark discussed the study with Wells.[25]

The *Study of the Effect of an Embargo of Trade between the United States and Japan* was prepared under the direction of Rear Admiral Richmond K. Turner. It reflected the belief that shutting off the American supply of petroleum would lead promptly to an invasion of the Netherlands East Indies. Although probable, this was not necessarily a certain and immediate result, because Japan, it was reasoned, had oil stocks for about eighteen months' war operations. If there were to be export restrictions on oil by the United States, they should be accompanied by similar restrictions by the British and Dutch. However, the results of a total embargo would be a severe psychological reaction against the United States and an intensification of determination of those in power in Japan to continue their present course. And then the words of prophecy:

> Further, it seems certain that, if Japan should then take military action against the British and Dutch, she would also include military action against the Philippines, which would immediately involve us in a Pacific war ... An embargo would probably result in a fairly early attack by Japan on Malaya and the Netherlands East Indies, and possibly would involve the United States in early war in the Pacific....

Recommendation: That trade with Japan not be embargoed at this time.[26]

On the copy of Admiral Turner's study, which was sent to Roosevelt, Stark wrote, "I concur in general. Is this the kind of picture you wanted?"[27] The President did not appear to have heeded the evaluations of Turner and Stark. His actions in ordering a freeze of Japanese assets on July 25 after the Japanese entered southern Indochina showed that he was less worried about immediate Japanese reaction against the United States than were his military advisers. As long as Britain stood, he thought, the Japanese would not enter the war, because they did not want to fight the British Empire and the United States together.[28]

The Navy, through the period of embargo considerations, was divided. The Secretary, and certain officers below the senior admirals, were for tight controls or even complete embargo. The Chief of Naval Operations, who had the advantage of personal contact with the President and who agreed with Sumner Welles, opposed actions which could result in war with Japan. For exactly one year they were able to influence Roosevelt against taking a harder stand. To the very end Stark held his position; he was so wrapped up in the problems of the Atlantic that he veered away from any action which would commit his limited number of ships to the Far East against Japan. Stark accepted the risk of allowing one very potential enemy to build up huge petroleum reserves in order to keep peace in one ocean while defeating an enemy considered more dangerous in another ocean.

CHAPTER 7

Allied Naval Strategy in the Pacific

The staff talks between British and American military planners in Washington in January 1941 had deep historical roots, since several of those instrumental in promoting the event had had experience in Anglo-American relations dating from World War I. Early in 1917, the First Lord of the Admiralty, Winston Churchill, had discussed with the United States ambassador, Walter Hines Page, the possibilities of a visit to London by an American admiral. Ultimately, Rear Admiral William S. Sims, president of the Naval War College, was sent as a United States naval observer to the Admiralty. His flag secretary, during his tour as the senior American naval officer in European waters was Lieutenant Commander Harold Raynesford Stark. Stark had brought his command, a flotilla of torpedo boats, from the Asiatic Station to work with the British forces in the Mediterranean Sea and English Channel.

Almost simultaneously with Churchill's return to power in May 1940 he made his request for American destroyers and his suggestion that the United States Fleet use Singapore as an advanced naval base. Temporarily failing to get satisfaction on his request for destroyers and having his suggestion on Singapore positively rejected, Churchill on June 15 appointed a special committee headed by Admiral Sir Sidney Bailey to improve relations with the United States. Admiral Bailey had retired in 1939 but was recalled to duty in the Admiralty for "miscellaneous and special assignments." The Bailey Committee's function was to review the form of American aid to be sought, the possible areas of British and American operations and the two fleets' responsibilities in those areas, the preferred policy of cooperation, and the techniques of imparting information to United States authorities.

Five days later the U.S. Naval Attache, Captain Alan G. Kirk, was advised that informal conversations between British and American staffs either in London or Washington were to be proposed. The Bailey Committee held meetings from June 20 to September 8, 1940, examining "each of the major technical aspects of future naval co-operation." It recommended at the July 15 meeting that cooperation with American naval authorities should conform closely to the 1917–1918 precedent.[1]

The pressure for naval cooperation was also exerted through the regular diplomatic channels. Lord Lothian, the British ambassador in Washington, recalling the World War I services of Admiral Sims, suggested to President Roosevelt in June 1940 the sending of another senior American admiral. Roosevelt liked the idea and discussed it with Secretary of the Navy Frank Knox and Admiral Stark. On July 12, they proposed Rear Admiral Robert Lee Ghormley, the Assistant Chief of Naval Operations and former head of the War Plans Division, who was already fully informed on the past conversations. Roosevelt, while briefing Ghormley prior to his departure for London, informed him that he "still was not convinced that the United States would be forced to intervene as a belligerent in the war against the European Axis, or would be forced to fight Japan in the Pacific to prevent continued Japanese expansion."[2] In addition to Ghormley, Roosevelt decided to send for a shorter period of time an Army representative, General George V. Strong. A third member was selected to represent the air arm, Major General Delos C. Emmons.

The trio arrived in London August 15 and were joined by the U.S. Naval Attache, Captain Kirk, and the U.S. Military Attache, Colonel Raymond E. Lee. The meetings with the British which ensued were referred to as "The Anglo-American Standardization of Arms Committee" although the discussions covered many matters of joint planning and possible cooperation, particularly on the part of the two fleets. The American delegation repeatedly stressed that they were present as individuals for discussion and recommendations, but this did not deter the British from "fielding their first military team" or from speaking with complete candor. In the British group were Admiral of the Fleet Sir Dudley Pound, First Sea Lord; General Sir John Dill, Chief of the Imperial General Staff; and Air Chief Marshall Sir Cyril L. N. Newall, Chief of the Air Staff. It was Sir Cyril Newall who gave the American visitors the crux of British strategic thinking at the time. Their plans for the future certainly relied on the continued economic and industrial cooperation of the United States in ever-increasing volume, but no account had been taken of the probability of active cooperation by the United States, since this was clearly a matter of high political policy. The economic and industrial cooperation of the United States were fundamental to their strategy.

Discussion relative to the Far East pointed up the fact that the earlier British assumptions were admittedly invalid relative to possible Japanese action. First, it had been assumed that the threat to British interests would be seaborne; second, that a fleet could be sent to the Far East. The Japanese now threatened to expand through the southeast in such a way as to make land invasion of Malaya possible; and the British were obviously in no position to send a fleet to the Far East. At this juncture, important as Singapore and Malaya were, they could not be supported at the cost of security in the Atlantic or the Mediterranean. The British position impressed the American delegation then and was to prove an area of disagreement later.

Generals Strong and Emmons continued on in London through the height of the German air attack which was to have defeated Britain. Impressed by the British coolness and determination under heavy attack, they returned to Washington the last part of September confident that Britain would stand—at least for the immediate future. Admiral Ghormley stayed on in London as a special naval observer.

Admiral Ghormley conferred almost daily with the Bailey Committee. The committee, on the assumption that the U.S. naval strength would be concentrated in the Pacific, had recommended that strong forces be moved into the Southwest Pacific and China Sea, in order to restrain Japanese movements to the south, and particularly into the Netherlands East Indies. Admiral Ghormley, in commenting on this recommendation, reviewed the problems that would be involved for the United States Navy in moving such detachments across the Pacific. He pointed out that the First Sea Lord and other officers of the naval staff had themselves suggested that the Royal Navy was not sufficiently strong in the Atlantic. Assistance from the United States Navy would probably be required in the Atlantic, in addition to whatever action might be taken in the Pacific. Admiral Ghormley referred to the existing strength of the U.S. Navy in the Atlantic. A large proportion of these naval forces would probably be needed to cooperate with the British in the Atlantic although this would depend upon developments in the relations with Japan and on the attitude which the administration and public opinion might take, should the United States enter the war.[3]

The revised text of the Bailey Committee reports were sent by Admiral Ghormley to Admiral Stark, with a record of the discussions which had been proceeding since September 17. Stark, in a dispatch of October 2, suggested that the naval attache return to Washington to be available for consultation there while these proposals were under consideration. Admiral Richardson, Commander in Chief, United States Fleet, was in Washington conferring on what to do with the fleet in the Pacific when Kirk received his orders to proceed to Washington for discussions in December concerning cooperation with the Admiralty. On October 14, 1940, after the United States had turned down once again the suggestion to send a strong detachment to Singapore, Lord Lothian presented Roosevelt with a proposal from Churchill for staff conversations on a "comprehensive basis." On October 16 in London Admiral Pound spoke to the same purpose in conversations with Ghormley. The Churchill proposal to deter the Japanese from taking counteractions to the reopening of the Burma Road was first confirmed by the White House, then, because of its political ramifications, denied. On October 27, Lord Lothian's memorandum was returned without action or further comment. Roosevelt had to win an election first before there could be even secret talks with the British strategists.

The temporary reluctance to conduct conversations with the British military leaders because of political liabilities and, concomitantly, Roosevelt's procrastination on reaching an agreement with his own military advisers on a national policy prompted Stark to try his hand at writing an estimate of the world situation. The initial purpose of this naval effort on November 4 was to arrive "at a decision as to the National Objective in order to facilitate naval preparation." Much of the strategic thought in the estimate came from Captain Richmond Kelly Turner, who had become head of the War Plans Division less than a month before. Turner had come from the staff of the Naval War College where, in April of that year, discussions of the world situation had led to certain conclusions which now became key elements in the November study in Washington—priority given to the defeat of Germany, aid to the democracies to hasten the defeat of Germany, and an initial defensive posture relative to Japan.[4] Stark's first rough notes were reviewed, debated, and revised by a group of his staff officers, most of whom would be renowned admirals in the future. In addition to Turner, Captain Royal Eason Ingersoll and Commander Charles Maynard Cooke, Jr., War Plans Division officer, and Commanders Forrest Percival Sherman and Oscar Charles Badger worked "day and night, Saturdays and Sundays, for about ten consecutive days"[5] on the paper.

The product of their joint effort, submitted as a memorandum

105

from the CNO to Secretary Knox on November 12, was undoubtedly one of the most important policy papers, if not the most important one, in the immediate pre-war years. It would ultimately become the basis for the American position in conversations with the British, would become the United States national war policy and the basis for *Rainbow 5*.

Initially, Stark analyzed the various ways by which the United States might become involved in the war. Shortly thereafter, he stated of the national objectives as he saw them:

> ... preservation of the territorial, economic, and ideological integrity of the United States, plus that of the remainder of the Western Hemisphere; the prevention of the disruption of the British Empire, with all that such a consummation implies; and the diminution of the offensive military power of Japan, with a view to the retention of our economic and political interests in the Far East.[6]

He rationalized why it was in the United States' interest to "prevent the disruption of the British Empire" and especially to ensure that the British Isles remained intact. The British Isles, the "Heart of the Empire," must remain intact as the "geographical positions from which successful land action can later be launched" against Germany. Second only to the British Isles in strategic importance were Egypt, and Gibraltar, combined with west and northwest Africa.

Various possible options of support to the British and Dutch forces in the Pacific were also discussed in depth, along with a thorough analysis of the shortcomings of the existing *Orange Plan*. The crux of the recommended policy in the Pacific was "a limited war against Japan" reducing her offensive power chiefly through economic blockade. To accomplish that blockade the

> ... allied strategy would comprise holding the Malay Barrier, denying access to other sources of supply in Malaysia, severing her lines of communication with the Western Hemisphere, and raiding communications to the Mid-Pacific, the Philippines, China, and Indo-China.[7]

The defensive strategy also called for reinforcement of army strength in Hawaii and Alaska, the establishment of naval bases in the Fiji, Samoan, and Gilbert islands and possibly reinforcing the Philippines with aircraft. Stark did not believe that "the British and Dutch alone could hold Malay Barrier without direct military assistance by the United States." He was convinced that "they would need in addition to the Asiatic Fleet further reenforcement by ships and aircraft drawn from the Fleet in Hawaii, and possibly even troops." All the Pacific options were weighed against their impact on Atlantic operations. Shifting the discussion back to the Atlantic, Stark reasoned that naval assistance alone would not *"assure* final victory for Great Britain," but that additionally it would be necessary "to send large air and land forces to Europe or Africa, or both, and to participate strongly in this land offensive."[8] Ironically, it was naval strategists who were advocating large U.S. land armies to defeat Germany.

Stark next presented most succinctly the necessity for deciding upon a national policy.

> With war in prospect, I believe our every effort should be directed toward the *prosecution of a national* policy with *mutually supporting diplomatic and military aspects,* and having as its guiding feature a determination that any intervention we may undertake shall be such as will ultimately best *promote our own national interests.* We should seek the best answer to the question: "Where should we fight the war, and for what objective?" With the answer to this question to guide me, I can make a more logical plan, can more appropriately distribute the naval forces, can better coordinate the future material preparation of the Navy, and can more usefully advise as to whether or not proposed diplomatic measures can adequately be supported by available naval strength.[9]

Having stated the urgency for a national policy decision, Stark presented four possible plans which could be considered feasible for the United States: (A) Western Hemisphere defense only; (B) full offensive against Japan and strictly defensive in the Atlantic; (C) the strongest possible military assistance both to the British in Europe and to the British, Dutch, and Chinese in the Far East; and (D) "eventual strong offensive in the Atlantic as an ally of the British and a defensive in the Pacific." This latter plan was the recommended course of action. Since, in the phonetic alphabet in use at the time, "D" was "Dog," the plan became known as *Plan Dog.*

Copies of *Plan Dog* were sent to General Marshall and Admirals Richardson and Ghormley. Through Ghormley a copy was shown informally to the Admiralty and Churchill. Long before Stark's recommendations were approved as the United States' position by Roosevelt or accepted by the United States Army, Churchill had, within his own circle of advisers, completely endorsed *Plan Dog.* On November 22, Churchill told his senior military officers:

> In my view Admiral Stark is right, and *Plan Dog* is strategically sound, and also most highly adapted to our interests. We should therefore, so far as opportunity serves, in every way contribute to strengthen

the policy Admiral Stark, and should not use arguments inconsistent
with it. . . .

I am much encouraged by the American naval view.[10]

The closing paragraph of *Plan Dog* certainly must have hit a re-
sponsive chord with the British staff. For months they had been pushing for conversations with their American counterparts. Stark's last
recommendation was for immediate secret staff talks on technical
matters with both the military and naval authorities—in London or
Washington with the British, in Washington with the Canadians, and
in Singapore or Batavia with the British and Dutch.

The proposed position for the United States as advanced by Admiral Stark was not completely acceptable to the other factions in the
decision-making scheme. The Army's War Plans Division staff generally
agreed with the emphasis of *Plan Dog* on British survival and the
necessity of American assistance to that end; however, they were most
definite in their stand of "making no commitments in the Far East."
Plan Dog, with the Army comments, was sent to Roosevelt on November 13. Receiving no answer, Stark and Marshall on November 18
directed the Joint Planning Committee to apply itself to drafting a
national policy acceptable to the Army and Navy which would meet
presidential approval. On November 29, General Marshall informed
Admiral Stark that the Army still could not accept the strategic concept of the war or the opinion set forth in the plan relative to the proposals concerning the Malay Barrier. Army planners thought United
States war plans should be based on the immediate goals of Britain's
survival, Germany's defeat, and concentration of "our power to operate effectively, decisively if possible, in the principal theater—the
Atlantic." As far as Malaysia was concerned, they thought the United
States should avoid dispersing its forces into that theater; however, it
should assist the British in reinforcing their naval forces in the Far
East by relieving them of naval obligations in the Atlantic. This
would provide a more homogeneous force for Malaysia and would, in
effect, concentrate rather than disperse American naval power.

Stark's answer to Marshall on the same day, November 29,
showed something of his pique with his Army associates and a veiled
indication of presidential omnipresent influence in strategy. He replied, "Should we become engaged in the war described in *Rainbow 3,*
it will not be through my doings, but because those in higher authority have decided that it is to our best national interest to accept
such a war."[11] In the same memorandum he also said, "I consider it

essential that we know a great deal more about British ideas than we have yet been able to glean."

Roosevelt in no way committed himself to the theory of strategy outlined in *Plan Dog* and whatever he said to Stark about his plan did not become a matter of record.[12] He did authorize conversations between representatives of the American and British staffs to explore the problems raised by Stark. Stark instructed Ghormley, whose exploratory conversations in London had reached the limit of their usefulness, to arrange with the British staffs for serious conversations to begin in Washington early the next year. Since Stark regarded the British ideas of American naval deployment in the Pacific as unacceptable, he told Ghormley to inform the Admiralty that anyone they sent to Washington "should have instructions to discuss concepts based on equality of considerations for both the United States and British Commonwealth, and to explore realistically the various fields of war cooperation." Impatient for an answer, Stark personally requested the First Sea Lord, Admiral of the Fleet Sir Dudley Pound, on November 30, to send accredited representatives to Washington before Christmas if that were possible. In reply to the initial invitation Admiral Ghormley, on December 2, announced the names of the British staff who were to come to Washington in January. Admiral Pound, in answering Stark's letter, assured the Chief of Naval Operations that the ideas already expressed by the Admiralty were not to be regarded as "an unalterable basis" of discussion.

The announcement of the British acceptance of the invitation to converse in Washington lent urgency to the determination of an agreed-upon military policy. The Joint Planning Committee reported to the Joint Board on December 21 on its study and offered a tentative draft of a joint memorandum to the President from the Secretaries of State, War, and Navy. Not unexpectedly, it emphasized the priority of operations in the Atlantic. The *Plan Dog* influence showed in the assertion that, although United States interests in the Far East were important, it was incorrect to consider them as important as the integrity of the Western Hemisphere, or as important as preventing the defeat of the British Commonwealth. The issues in the Orient would largely be decided in Europe. The final proposed recommendations were a rapid increase in military and naval strength, concomitant with not provoking an attack by any other power and not willingly engaging in any war with Japan. If forced into a war with Japan, Pacific operations should be restricted to permit use of forces for a major offensive in the Atlantic. Finally, no important Allied decision should be accepted without a clear understanding "as to common objectives, as to contingents to be provided, as to operations planned, and as to command arrangements."[13]

Secretary Hull declined to approve the proposed recommendations since he doubted the propriety of his joining in recommendations to the President concerning technical military statements. Out of the conference over the State Department's acceptance of the policy, a long-overdue change in the upper echelon liaison became effective. Hull suggested, and it was agreed, that the three secretaries would meet each Tuesday on national defense matters, thus superseding the Liaison Committee of Sumner Welles and the military representatives.

The written record does not show the rationale leading to the event, but it is reasonable to assume that the calling of the three secretaries, the Chief of Naval Operations, and the Chief of Staff to the White House on January 16 was prompted by the immediately past discussions on national and military policy. Also, the President, as recorded by General Marshall the next day, had in mind the possibilities of sudden and simultaneous action on the part of Germany and Japan against the United States. He felt that there was one chance in five of such an eventuality, and that it might culminate any day. He devoted himself principally to a discussion of the United States' attitude in the Far East towards Japan and to the matter of curtailment of American shipments of war supplies to Britain. He thought that, in the event of hostile action by Germany and Japan, Churchill should be notified immediately that this would not curtail the supply of material to Britain. The final directive from the President was that the United States would stand on the defensive in the Pacific with the fleet based on Hawaii; that the Commander in Chief, Asiatic Fleet, would have discretionary authority as to how long he could remain based in the Philippines and as to his direction of withdrawal —to the east or to Singapore; that there would be no naval reinforcement of the Philippines; that the Navy should have under consideration the possibility of bombing attacks against Japanese cities; that the Army should not be committed to any aggressive action until it was fully prepared to undertake it; that every effort be made to continue the supply of material to Britain and to disappoint Hitler's principal objective of involving the United States in a war at that particular time.[14]

Meanwhile the Joint Planning Committee, at the suggestion of Admiral Turner, had been directed on December 11 to draw up instructions for the United States Army and Navy representatives for holding conversations with the British staff due to arrive the next month. The report was submitted to the Joint Board initially on January 13, 1941, and after additional work again on January 21. After criticizing most of the recent leadership in Britain, the basic report gave a general evaluation of probable British proposals. The joint planners asserted that the United States was capable of safeguarding the North American continent, and probably the Western Hemisphere, whether allied with Britain or not, and it could not afford to entrust its national future to British direction. Military planners unanimously agreed that Britain could not defeat Germany unless the United States provided direct military assistance to a far greater degree than had been given so far and that, even then, success against the Axis was not assured. They expected that proposals of the British representatives would have been drawn up with chief regard for the support of the British Commonwealth and protection of their postwar commercial and military interests. The United States likewise should safeguard its own eventual interests. To avoid commitment by the President, the joint planners recommended that neither he nor any member of his cabinet should officially receive the British officers, but that they be informally received by the under secretary of state, and the service chiefs. [15]

The enclosure to the basic report on the forthcoming conversations contained agenda items and a clear statement of United States intentions. It was approved verbatim by the military chiefs and forwarded to Roosevelt via the service secretaries. On January 26, he sent a memorandum to the Secretary of the Navy with minor changes recommended. He thought the procedure was "all right." Taking a page out of the book of President Woodrow Wilson, under whom he had served as an assistant secretary of the Navy, Roosevelt preferred to use the term "associates" rather than "allies" in reference to possible future relationships between the United States and Britain. The planners had used a clause, "should the United States decide to resort to war." Roosevelt changed "decide" to "be compelled." His only other change was to modify the assistance to be given in the Mediterranean to read "navally."[16]

The purpose of the conversations with the British, as finally agreed upon, was "to determine the best methods by which the armed forces of the United States and the British Commonwealth [could] defeat Germany and the powers allied with her, should the United States be compelled to resort to war." The national position of the United States closely paralleled *Plan Dog*. It was to "defend the Western

Hemisphere, aid the British Commonwealth against Germany; and oppose by diplomatic means any extension of Japanese rule over additional territory." Additionally, the two countries should "endeavor to keep Japan from entering the war or attacking the Dutch," but should Japan enter the war, "the United States operations in the mid-Pacific and the Far East would be conducted in such a manner as to facilitate the exertion of its principal military effort in the Atlantic or navally in the Mediterranean."[17]

The selected agenda items with which the conversations were to be concerned were indicative of the keen appreciation of possible political repercussions from any agreement. The descriptive term applied to the conversations (by Captain Ingersoll in London in January 1938 and Stark in *Plan Dog*) was "on technical matters," and the connotation of "technical" was a very restrictive "military." Considerations, the nature of which required obvious decisions by the heads of government, were "political" and consequently ruled out of the purview of the military planners. Although joint military plans, *per se,* have political significance when executed or made public, as in a threat to use same, joint preliminary planning may be readily accomplished in a strictly "military" sense. Under certain stated assumptions, *with no political decisions required,* military representatives may draw up quite intricate disposition plans, command arrangements, tasks assignments, etc. Such were the rules to be followed in the joint talks with the British. As added warranties to guarantee the maintenance of the "military" status, no member of the government was to be present and no cabinet official would formally receive the visitors. (Originally Sumner Welles, under secretary of state, was to have informally welcomed the group, but neither he nor any other government official actually was present at the first meeting.) Though the military services were each represented by senior officers, they were not the highest in any case, so the requirement for approval by higher authority was tacitly understood throughout the talks. The American military chiefs absented themselves after the initial meeting.

The flexibility enjoyed by the military planners in this case was unique. In essence, they could make plans which were not binding on either side and yet were detailed enough to be the basis for effective cooperation when approved by their respective political superiors. The planners likewise were not bound in the scope of their conversations to a rigid policy position which would have been inherent if the participants included political representatives or the senior military leaders.

During the interim period between the announcement on December 2, 1940, of the British intention to come to Washington and their departure from Britain, neither Admiral Ghormley nor Brigadier General Raymond Lee, the United States military attache in London, was able to get any advance information on the British position. The British explanation was logical and simple—it would jeopardize the security of their war plans to give the information at that time. The long list of questions posed by Ghormley and Lee solicited information desired by their respective services' war plans division in Washington. The list included questions on British strength and capabilities in the different areas of the world, on the relative importance of those areas in their strategic thinking, and what their proposed courses of action would be under certain conditions. The questions were answered in detail and made available to the Americans after the party left Britain.

On January 29, 1941, Chief of Naval Operations Stark and Army Chief of Staff Marshall welcomed the British delegation in a room set aside for the meetings in the Main Navy Building in Washington. The United States representatives were:

Major General S. D. Embick, Army representative on the Permanent Joint Board Defense (Canada-United States)

Brigadier General Sherman Miles, acting Assistant Chief of Staff, G-2

Brigadier General L. T. Gerow, head of the Army War Plans Division

Colonel J. T. McNarney, an air officer

Rear Admiral R. L. Ghormley, special observer in London

Rear Admiral R. K. Turner, head of Navy War Plans Division

Captain A. G. Kirk, assistant to Rear Admiral Turner and former naval attache in London

Lieutenant Colonel O. T. Pfeiffer, U.S. Marine Corps

The British representatives were:

Rear Admiral R. H. Bellairs, head of the British delegation

Rear Admiral V. H. Danckwerts

Major General E. L. Morris

Air Force Marshall J. C. Slessor, of the British Purchasing Commission in Washington

Captain A. W. Clarke, assistant naval attache in Washington

The Secretariat included:

Lieutenant Colonel W. P. Scobey, U.S. Army

Commander L. R. McDowell, U.S. Navy

Lieutenant Colonel A. T. Cornwall-Jones, British Army[18]

The American military leaders presented their position, which had been approved by the President, and then stressed the urgency for secrecy, especially in the light of the proposed Lend-Lease Act which was then being discussed in Congress. The British replied that they had come as a corporate body representing the British chiefs of staff, that they had complete freedom to discuss the general strategic position and to consider dispositions in the event the United States should enter the war.[19] In their opening talk the British gave a clear summation of their views and three propositions of general strategic policy:

> The European theatre is the vital theatre where a decision must first be sought.
>
> The general policy should therefore be to defeat Germany and Italy first, and then deal with Japan.
>
> The security of the Far Eastern position, including Australia and New Zealand, is essential to the cohesion of the British Commonwealth and to the maintenance of its war effort. Singapore is the key to the defence of these interests and its retention must be assured.[20]

The first two propositions were in direct accord with American feelings; the retention of Singapore certainly was not. The British repeatedly had told American representatives since the June 1940 visit of Lieutenant Commander Hampton of the Admiralty that they were unable to send major forces to the Far East. Their proposition amounted to an open invitation for the United States to defend Singapore. The policy to retain Singapore in the face of mounting Japanese power and British maneuverings to gain American acceptance of the idea became formidable obstacles upon which the meetings almost foundered. The British saw Singapore as more than just a military base. For political, economic, and psychological reasons it was a symbol of British Commonwealth unity and security in the Far East. Thus, for many reasons, it was part of British strategic thinking, and they never were to give up trying to make it part of British-American strategic plans.

Churchill's message on May 15, 1940 might be considered one starting point in the Singapore controversy, though to be sure Singapore had been discussed with Captain Ingersoll in January 1938. Roosevelt had wisely dodged the offer "to use Singapore in any way convenient." As a compromise the United States Fleet had been ordered to remain at Pearl Harbor shortly thereafter. On October 4, Churchill again wrote to Roosevelt mentioning the possibility of war with Japan over the re-opening of the Burma Road and the fact that

Japan had joined the Tripartite Pact. He asked at that time if it were possible to send "an American squadron, the bigger the better, to pay a friendly visit to Singapore." As a further suggestion, Churchill thought the occasion of the visit could be used for "technical discussion of naval and military problems in those and Philippine waters, and the Dutch might be invited to join."[21] Admiral Stark opposed the suggestions and even the reinforcement of the Asiatic Fleet because of the situation in the Atlantic. Roosevelt once again agreed with his naval advisers.

With such a past history of British proposals on Singapore, it was not surprising that the American planners would be wary of similar proposals at the Washington meetings. At the sixth Plenary Meeting on February 10, 1941, the situation in the Far East was the chief subject discussed. The British again emphasized their concern over the future status of Singapore. They urged that the United States should take early action both to keep Japan out of the war and to assure the defense of Singapore against a Japanese attack.[22] The proposal at this time was that the United States should send four heavy cruisers, an aircraft carrier, planes, and submarines to Singapore. The next day the British presented a detailed paper: *The Far East—Appreciation by the U. K. Delegation.* At the same time that the paper was being presented to the American military participants, Lord Halifax, the new British ambassador, was communicating its substance to Secretary of State Hull.[23]

The British paper pictured Singapore as a symbol of British ability and determination to protect the dominions and colonies and their trade with Britain. The loss of Singapore would greatly weaken the power of political leaders in Australia, New Zealand, India, and China who believed in the value of British friendship. The British representatives admitted that even if Singapore was lost, Australia and New Zealand could be held and the Japanese kept out of the Indian Ocean; the British insisted, however, that Singapore was a necessary "card of re-entry" when the European war should have taken a turn for the better. Without the base at Singapore, a successful attack against the Japanese would have to be launched across thousands of miles of ocean, either from India or Australia. In short, the British stand on Singapore was based "not only upon purely strategic foundations, but on political, economic and sentimental considerations which, even if not literally vital on a strictly academic view, are of such fundamental importance to the British Commonwealth that they must always be taken into serious account."[24] What the British delegation could not say specifically and what was obvious to the Americans was that the prestige of the British Empire in the Far East and at home was at stake.

The seriousness with which the British held to the Singapore position is shown by two key statements in the subject paper:

(a) The security of the Far Eastern position, including Australia and New Zealand, is essential to the maintenance of the war effort of the Associated Powers. Singapore is the key to the defense of these interests and its retention must be assured.

(b) If Singapore were in serious danger of capture, and the United States still withheld their aid, we should be prepared to send a Fleet to the Far East, even if to do so would compromise or sacrifice our position in the Mediterranean.[25]

The loss of Singapore, in the opinion of the British chiefs of staff, "would be a disaster of the first magnitude, second only to the loss of the British Isles."[26]

On February 13, U.S. Army and Navy representatives met to discuss the British paper. Rear Admiral Turner reviewed the background of the British proposals that had begun two and a half years before when "the President and Secretary of State more or less committed the United States Fleet to actions in conjunction with the British forces in the Far East." He observed that when Ingersoll was in London, in January 1938, the British proposed that the "United States send their whole fleet to Singapore and that the then combined United States and British forces should start a campaign against the Japanese." The British two years later were unable to send a strong force to the Far East, "but still would like the United States to send their whole fleet, together with a large United States Army, to engage against the Japanese." It was not until the last staff conversations that "they modified their requests for reenforcements to a force of four heavy cruisers, aircraft and submarines." Despite Stark's caution to Pound before the talks started and Pound's response that the British ideas were not to be regarded as "unalterable," it was now apparent to the American delegation

(a) That a concerted drive was being made by the British to influence the United States into accepting the British point of view in reference to the Far East situation.

(b) That the United Kingdom, while accepting the United States' Staff Committee's decision not to send the Pacific Fleet to the Far East, continues to push their requests for United States' commitments in that theater.

Major General Embick suggested that it was the duty of the United States delegation, as military advisers to the President, to present to him sound military opinion with reference to the Far East strategic situation with a suggested course of action.[27]

At this juncture the American delegation became quite perturbed upon learning of the Halifax-Hull discussion of the British military paper on the Far East. To have their own Secretary of State learn from a foreign diplomat about the controversial Singapore question was embarrassing, for the Americans had rigidly adhered to the "military" nature of the talks by not informing the State Department of the nature or progress of the joint meetings. To have the same unilaterally originated paper used in preliminary military talks discussed at the highest diplomatic levels violated a cardinal premise upon which the conversations were to take place. A protest was officially registered with the British delegation that the action appeared to the Americans to be an attempt to secure political pressure to influence their decision on Singapore.

One should remember, before condemning the British action, that the British military group in Washington was the best source of military information and strategy the British ambassador had in the country and, conversely, the ambassador was the highest government representative in the area to whom the military could refer. The exchange of information between the British representatives in Washington was certainly understandable; the use to which the ambassador put information so gained was the crux of the objection.

The British delegation replied to the protest and their answer was discussed by the Navy section of the United States staff delegation on February 20. Rear Admiral Ghormley stated that he thought their reply had clarified "the situation to the point wherein the plenary conversations could be resumed." Rear Admiral Turner wanted to take a much harder line. He wanted assurances that no United Kingdom delegation papers would be sent to the State Department and that, in addition, none of the United Kingdom delegation points developed in the course of conversations should be presented orally to the State Department through diplomatic channels. Staff conversations were to have been "on a purely military plane," and when concluded would become the basis "for sound military decisions representing, in the considered judgment of the combined membership, the best measures to be undertaken for the successful prosecution of the war." Until such joint decisions were reached, the presentation by British diplomats to the State Department of any matter under discussion tended to induce the latter to arrive at incorrect conclusions which would be difficult to change, since the United States delegation was not furnishing the State Department with its own views.[28]

Although the United States Navy representatives, especially Turner, thought that the British delegation was not playing the game fairly, further open conflict over the Singapore question ceased in the Washington conversations after presentation of *The United States Military Position in the Far East* on February 19. The Americans admitted that the loss of symbolic Singapore would be a serious blow, but it did not follow that serious blows always lead to final disaster. The common basis of American-British strategy was the security of the British Isles and control of the North Atlantic. Rather bluntly the British were told that they would have to do the best they could in protecting their interests elsewhere. The United States contribution was to eliminate the German threat to the British Isles and the North Atlantic.

Admiral Stark, who had been kept informed of the various stages of the discussions, felt that the whole question of policy to be followed by the United States in the Far East should be submitted to the President. In view of the disagreements of the United States and British delegations as to the strategic concepts which should govern any plan for combined action in the Far East, it seemed necessary to him that in any policy discussions between the State Department and the British ambassador, or between the President and the Prime Minister, the views of the American naval staff should be clearly understood.[29]

It soon became apparent that Admiral Stark's views on the importance of defeating Germany first continued to enjoy Roosevelt's approval. The *Plan Dog* concept was the touchstone of the "position" paper given to the British on February 19, and the "President informed the Chief of Naval Operations and the Chief of Staff of his approval of the position adopted by the American Delegation in the Staff Conference." He further agreed that this position was in conformity with the Stark memorandum of November 12 (*Plan Dog*).[30]

Singapore had become a dead issue in the American-British conversations (ABC). The final report, called *ABC-1*,[31] was finished on March 27, 1941. The basic report reiterated the general policy positions of the two governments, dealing almost exclusively with the Atlantic conflict. The two key paragraphs pertaining to Japan are significant. The first mentioned neither Japan nor Singapore, though the actions of the former and the importance of the latter had recently been argued.

The security of the United Kingdom must be maintained in all cir-cumstances. Similarly, the United Kingdom, the Dominions, and India must maintain dispositions which, in all eventualities, will provide for the ultimate security of the British Commonwealth. A cardinal feature of British strategic policy is the *retention of a position in the Far East* such as will ensure the cohesion and security of the British Common-wealth and the maintenance of its war effort.[32] (Emphasis supplied.)

The second paragraph was the only subdivision of ten which mentioned Japan under a heading: "Plans for the Military operations of the Associated Powers will likewise be governed by the following:"

(d)   Even if Japan were not initially to enter the war on the side of the Axis Powers, it would still be necessary for the Associated Powers to deploy their forces in a manner to guard against eventual Japanese intervention. If Japan does enter the war, the Mili-tary strategy in the Far East will be defensive. The United States does not intend to add to its present Military strength in the Far East but will employ the United States Pacific Fleet offensively in the manner best calculated to weaken Japanese economic power, and to *support* the defense of the Malay barrier *by diverting Jap-anese strength away from Malaysia*. The United States intends so to augment its forces in the Atlantic and Mediterranean areas that the British Commonwealth will be in a position to release the necessary forces for the Far East.[33] (Emphasis supplied.)

Annex 3 to *ABC-1* was a United States-British Commonwealth Joint Basic War Plan. Forces and tasks were assigned by areas and by countries. Under tasks assigned American naval forces in the Pacific were:

(a)   Support the forces of the Associated Powers in the Far East by diverting enemy strength away from the Malay Barrier through the denial and capture of positions in the Marshalls, and through raids on enemy communications and positions.

(b)   Destroy Axis sea communications by capturing or destroying vessels trading directly with the enemy.

(c)   Protect the sea communications of the Associated Powers within the Pacific Area.

(d)   Support British naval forces in the area south of the Equator, as far west as Longitude 155° East.

(e)   Protect the territory of the Associated Powers within the Pacific Area, and prevent the extension of enemy Military power into the Western Hemisphere, by destroying hostile expeditions and by sup-porting land and air forces in denying the enemy the use of land positions in that Hemisphere.

(f) Prepare to capture and establish control over the Caroline and Marshall Island area.[34]

In the Far East Area the American naval tasks were generally the same as in the Pacific Area—raids, destroying communications, and attacking vessels. A "Special Command Relationships" section was included which would promote more plans and disagreements in the months ahead. The pertinent parts were:

30. The defense of the territories of the Associated Powers in the Far East Area will be the responsibility of the respective Commanders of the Military forces concerned. These Commanders will make such arrangements for mutual support as may be practicable and appropriate.

31. In the Far East Area the responsibility for the strategic direction of naval forces of the Associated Powers, except of naval forces engaged in supporting the defense of the Philippines, will be assumed by the British Commander in Chief, China. The Commander in Chief, United States Asiatic Fleet, will be responsible for the direction of naval forces engaged in supporting the defense of the Philippines.

32. The British Naval Commander in Chief, China, is also charged with responsibility for the strategic direction of the naval forces of the Associated Powers operating in the Australia and New Zealand Area.[35]

The guide lines for conversations between the British and American commanders in chief in the Far East have been stated here. How they were followed will be discussed in the next chapter.

The associations of the British and American navies had reached a high point in World War I when the United States supported Britain in the defeat of Germany. Certainly another high point was the agreements reached in *ABC-1*. Discussions had covered strategic concepts, objectives, and the exchange of information on forces to meet those objectives. A basic war plan had been produced and general tasks assigned primarily to defeat Germany using American forces, should the United States be "compelled to resort to war." The problems in the Pacific were not so neatly resolved. The thinking there was defensive, with each government responsible for the defense of its own territories. Despite the positiveness of the American position on the Singapore question in February and the fact that there would be no reinforcement of the Asiatic Fleet, latitude was still given for discussions on mutual support between the on-scene commanders in chief.

The evolution of cooperation in the Pacific between the British and Americans was not complete with *ABC-1,* but it had reached a "point of no return." The United States was irrevocably tied to Britain in two oceans: in the Atlantic, to defeat a European enemy; in the Pacific to stand defensively against an Asiatic enemy. In both, the use of the U.S. Navy was most important, and in the Pacific beyond Hawaii it was the only American force ready for use. *ABC-1* immediately became the basis for United States War Plan *Rainbow 5* and the matrix against which future agreements in Singapore would be compared and rejected.

CHAPTER 8

American-British-Dutch Defense Plans

The general guidelines for Anglo-American cooperation in the Pacific and Far Eastern areas were cautiously agreed upon as part of the *ABC* conversations in Washington in March 1941. After the near-catastrophic schism in the discussions over the issue of Singapore, the participants had settled on words which in and of themselves left no doubt that the United States would not commit forces from its Pacific Fleet to defend Far Eastern territories—either territories belonging to others or even its own Philippine Islands.

> The United States does not intend to add to its present Military strength in the Far East but will employ the United States Pacific Fleet offensively in the manner best calculated to weaken Japanese economic power, and to support the defense of the Malay barrier by diverting Japanese strength away from Malaysia.[1]

Later there appeared the words: "The defense of the territories of the Associated Powers in the Far East Area [was] the responsibility of the respective commander of the military forces concerned." Immediately following these words of finality was the caveat that these "commanders will make such arrangements for mutual support as may be practicable and appropriate." Put in proper historical perspective, these few words advocating arrangements for mutual support in the Far East told the story of an elusive goal spanning years before their *ABC* enunciation and continuing to within hours of the long-dreaded and finally executed Japanese attack.

As early as the fall of 1936 when Admiral Yarnell assumed duty as Commander in Chief, Asiatic Fleet, he observed that the British officers were concerned over the United States withdrawing "protec-

122

tion from that gateway to Singapore and India" by granting independence to the Philippines and leaving them to their political fate. Senior British officers in the Far East at that time thought that the "Japanese menace could only be met with British-American cooperation and that the Japanese projected 'southward expansion policy' could be prevented by a strong naval base in the Philippines plus the Singapore base."[2] Yarnell made his impact on future American thinking relative to the Far East when in September 1939, he reasoned with Admiral Stark, the Chief of Naval Operations that since the United States would never build a "first class naval base in the Philippines" it should never engage Japan singlehandedly. "Great Britain, France and the Netherlands are vitally interested and should take part." Yarnell was not given the authority, nor did he seek it, to reach agreements with the other European powers to contain an advance by Japan south of China. Those tenuous agreements that were reached were achieved, not in the Far East, but in London in January 1938 as a result of Captain Ingersoll's visit with the Admiralty. The agreement to cooperate with naval forces was cast aside in 1939 when Germany threatened Europe.

In February 1940, Admiral Stark quoted Yarnell when he passed his words of advice across the Pacific to Yarnell's successor, Admiral Hart. Hart was told that the United States should never start "anything in the Western Pacific unless the principally interested powers (United States-French-British-Dutch) act in concert." Nevertheless, Stark thought the "possibility of getting such concerted action" to be improbable due to the "unpredictable state of affairs in Europe." Despite the improbability of cooperation Stark's planners were considering the use of Hong Kong, Singapore, North Borneo, or French or Dutch possessions in concerted actions, but they were not sure any of them would be available.[3]

Uncertainty in February 1940, over the availability of bases in the Far East was nothing compared to the uncertainty of Japanese actions vis-à-vis the Netherlands East Indies after Germany occupied the Netherlands in May. To a slightly lesser degree there was uncertainty over Japanese reaction to the embargoes imposed by the United States in July. There was genuine fear, which became stronger with each week in the early fall of 1940, that Japan would move swiftly against the Netherlands East Indies or the Philippines and Guam or against all of them. In September the Joint Planning Committee recommended to the Chief of Naval Operations and the Chief of Staff that if the United States were confronted with the necessity of armed

123

opposition to Japan, the effort should "be limited to the employment of minor naval surface and air forces operating from Singapore and Dutch East Indies bases, plus the interruption of Japanese shipping in the eastern Pacific."[4]

In line with the thoughts in Washington on cooperative action in the Far East against the Japanese threat, Admiral Hart sent his assistant chief of staff, Commander Frank Pugh Thomas, to Singapore for preliminary talks with the British military commanders in October. Thomas returned to Manila—where Hart had the bulk of the Asiatic Fleet—with a copy of the British Far Eastern War Plan. In time the plan was forwarded to Washington where Stark commented that it showed the usual British wishful thinking.

Meanwhile from London came another report of British wishful thinking. Rear Admiral Ghormley, the special naval observer, who was in daily contact with the Bailey Committee and other admiralty members, reported the British to be expectant of active American participation in the war now that Roosevelt had been reelected. They talked about the defense of the Malay Barrier and an "alliance between themselves, us, and the Dutch, without much thought as to what the effect would be in Europe."[5]

Stark, who relayed the information from Ghormley to Hart, had no idea whether the British would immediately fight if the Dutch alone, or the United States, alone, were attacked by the Japanese. Furthermore, although he believed the Dutch colonial authorities would resist an attempt to capture their islands, he questioned whether they would fight if only the Philippines, or only Singapore, were attacked. Hart was told that the Navy could make no political commitments, consequently, he could make no specific military plans for an allied war. However, Hart could perform a useful service "by laying with the British and possibly the Dutch, a framework for a future plan of cooperation," should the United States be forced into the war. Stark doubted that the Dutch would talk freely with Hart, but if they would, he should explore the fields of "command arrangements, general objectives, general plan of cooperative action, including the approximate naval and military deployment."[6]

Stark's letter to Hart, written on November 12, contained the first indication of optimism over immediate Japanese actions. Stark believed that Japan would avoid hostilities with the United States and it was doubtful at that time that she wished to fight the British and the Dutch. However, if a war developed between Japan and an alliance of the United States, Britain, and the Netherlands, Stark's ver-

sion of the allied objective was economic starvation and the holding
of a blockade along the Malay Barrier. (This was written the same
day *Plan Dog* was finished.) Then followed a definite promise of assistance to Hart which would be positively reversed four months later
in the *ABC* conversations:

> One thing (and this is for your ears alone) you can depend upon is
> that we would support you, probably by sending a naval reenforcement
> to you at Soerabaja or Singapore, and by other means.[7]

Hart was also told that the Navy's part of *Rainbow 3* was nearing
completion and would be sent "within a short time." That was the
plan which called for securing control of the western Pacific as
rapidly as possible. Stark planned to send *Rainbow 3* to Hart via one
of the naval attaches recently approved for Singapore, Ceylon, and
three ports in the Netherlands East Indies: Soerabaja (Surabaja) and
Batavia (Djakarta) in Java and Balikpapan in Borneo.

A month later Stark forwarded two copies of *Rainbow 3* to Hart
stressing the "possible eventuality" of war with Germany, Japan, and
Italy and directing that high priority be given to operating plans and
the preparation of vessels, aircraft, and personnel. One of the assumptions of the plan was that the United States would fight the war,
having Britain and the Netherlands Colonial Authorities as allies.
Staff conversations with the British had already been scheduled to
commence in Washington the next month, yet Stark considered that
the only useful staff conversations concerning an allied operating
plan and command arrangements in the Far East would be those
which the Commander in Chief, Asiatic Fleet, might be able to hold
with the British and Dutch supreme war commanders in that area.
Again he stated his belief that Hart might be able to hold such conversations with the British, but he had considerable doubt "as to the
extent of the conversations which may become possible with the
Dutch, owing to their fear of repercussions in Japan." He authorized
Hart to conduct staff conversations with the British and Dutch supreme commanders, with the specific understanding that he was in
no way to commit the United States government to any particular
political or military decisions, and that the purpose of the staff conversations was solely to facilitate joint operations should "war even-
tuate under the approximate conditions shown in the assumptions of
Rainbow 3." Hart was further cautioned to conduct his discussions in
secret, taking particular care not to permit the Japanese to learn of
the efforts to establish contact with the Dutch.[8]

Captain William Reynolds Purnell, chief of staff to Admiral Hart, had attended a British-Dutch meeting in Singapore in December when Stark's letter to Hart arrived, directing more talks with the Dutch. From January 10 to 14, Purnell conferred with Vice Admiral C. E. L. Helfrich and his staff in Batavia on possible joint defensive actions against the Japanese southward movements. The Dutch feared an attack by Japan and were highly desirous of any support. That support did not appear to be forthcoming from the British authorities in Singapore whose interest, one Dutch committeeman caustically remarked, dwindled as the scene moved eastward from Singapore.[9] Captain Purnell asked what steps the Dutch would take in case the Japanese attacked Singapore, and was told that the British and Netherlands had not given each other guarantees of mutual help. The Singapore conferences had made a proposal to the two governments, that if the Japanese moved in force south of the 6° North parallel, the British and Netherlands East Indies forces would be free to attack them without further declaration of war. The Netherlands government had rejected the proposal and the decision of the British government was unknown.

Captain Purnell was asked two major questions: first, what action would the United States take in case of a Japanese attack against the Netherlands East Indies coming through the Sulu Sea, and second, what would the United States do about the protection of shipping from the East Indies to the West Coast of the United States in case of a Japanese-N.E.I. war, the United States remaining neutral? To the first query Captain Purnell replied that the United States would guarantee the neutrality of the Philippines to the extent of attacking with all forces available, would notify Japan as well as all other nations of serious breaches of neutrality, and would probably maintain a benevolent neutrality toward the Dutch and British. To the second question he replied that he thought a war zone would be prescribed and that conditions would be the same as existed then in European waters. As an entirely personal view he stated that he believed the United States would take the necessary step to protect shipping, or to secure the materials, if the loss of the materials would seriously hamper United States production. When asked if he thought the United States would go to war with Japan if she attacked the Netherlands East Indies, he stated, emphasizing it was his own personal view, he thought she would.[10] The Netherlands authorities reciprocated by furnishing Purnell with detailed information on their naval and air strengths, and the status of their facilities, ports, bases, and storage areas.

In mid-February, when the question of defending Singapore was warming up the American and British staff conversations in Washington, another British-Dutch meeting in Singapore was announced to begin on February 22. Stark directed Hart to have his representative participate with the other two powers' representatives in order to agree on a joint plan of operations for the United States, British, and Dutch forces, but without making any political commitments. Any agreements were to be subject to Hart's and Stark's approval. Rules to be followed by the Asiatic Fleet representative were to "include provisions for a common acceptance of equality of political, economic and military control and be based on the use of only the forces now" in the Asiatic Fleet. Strategic plans adopted were to be fully realistic, and to this end the United States representative was told to express Stark's "view that British and Dutch strategic arrangements which depend for their efficacy upon intervention by the United States would not be sound, since there is doubt that Congress would declare war in case of Japanese aggression against powers other than the United States." Stark acknowledged that his instruction put Hart in "a difficult position but more definite instructions" could not be given to him.[11]

Two weeks later Admiral Hart reported to the Chief of Naval Operations the disappointing results of this latest attempt to develop a definite agreement without American guarantees of cooperation. That which the naval leaders sought and did not get was a strategic plan of operations against the Japanese in which the United States would participate if it should be "compelled to resort to war" against Japan—something similar to *ABC-1* in the Atlantic relative to Germany.

Specifically, the purpose of the conference was to agree upon an Anglo-Dutch-Australian plan—the first step. Present were separate representatives of the army, navy and air arms for Britain and Australia and of the army and navy for the Netherlands. Certain agreements were reached for cooperative action subject to the approval of their respective governments, but according to Captain Purnell, the United States representative, they "didn't really get down to cases enough . . . They *all*, except for some Dutch promises, have altogether a defensive attitude on water as well as on shore. . . . Their navies are now intended primarily for guarding their own ship lanes—not at all for going after the enemy's . . ." Yet Purnell was convinced that the British and Dutch *local* navies, but not the Australian-New Zealand navies, would do whatever the United States asked if they felt their own sea supply and reinforcement lines were reasonably secure and if the United States made a definite commitment toward participation. That commitment of course could not be given, and the disappointment expressed by Admiral Hart and reechoed in Washington would prove to be the rule rather than the exception relative to other Singapore talks. At the end of Hart's letter, which transmitted the latest Purnell report, he asked Stark to think over the advisability of the Asiatic Fleet's making "a Netherlands East Indies cruise just as a matter of peacetime course, something that has been done in former years."[12]

Admiral Hart's letter reporting the lack of progress being made in the Far East planning scheme arrived as the *ABC-1* plan was nearing completion. The Far East agreements had been sought to complement the Washington talks, and the unfavorable report prompted Stark to attempt corrective action. Copies of Hart's letter were sent to the President and the Secretary of State in the belief that a word from each of them "may do much toward getting the British, the Dutch, the Australians and the New Zealanders together." Stark assured Roosevelt that the Navy would do what it could toward this end. In the same memorandum Stark endorsed Hart's idea for the Netherlands East Indies cruise, provided it was properly timed. He liked the idea, because it was "the most positive move" the Asiatic Fleet could make; it was in line with United States war plans, so if war were to break, the Navy "would be sitting with [its] surface ships where [it] wanted them." Stark mentioned that sometime ago Hart had asked permission to pay a visit to Hong Kong with his flagship, and like the present proposal, Stark thought it was a good move. That visit was vetoed in deferrence to the objections of the State Department, as was this last one.[13]

The agreements in the *ABC-1 Report* were reached with the full approval of Admiral Stark and General Marshall, who, though not in attendance at the meetings, kept currently informed on the staff conversations. As a result of the accord with the British in Washington, the Joint Planning Committee was given a new directive for the preparation of the joint basic plan, *Rainbow 5,* "based upon the report of the United States British Staff Conversations, dated 27 March 1941 (*ABC-1*) and upon the Canadian-United States Basic Defense Plan No. 2 (*ABC-22*)." Stark and Marshall took steps immediately to implement the *ABC-1* agreement by arranging for detailed planning within the War and Navy Department staff and commands to conform to the agreement. Instructions were also sent to Major General

George Grunert, commanding general of the Philippine Department, and Admiral Hart—the two senior United States officers in the Far East—"to complete arrangements with the British and Dutch Commands for a Far Eastern Staff Conference at Singapore at as early a date as possible."[14]

On April 2, General Marshall sent by courier a complete copy of the *ABC-1* report to Grunert to permit advance planning with Commander in Chief, Asiatic Fleet, and Commandant Sixteenth Naval District. Grunert was specifically ordered not "to discuss" the matter with the British and Dutch commands. On April 4, the restriction not "to discuss" was revoked by a message from Marshall that a conference had been called in Singapore.[15]

A parallel message from Admiral Stark to Admiral Hart was sent on April 5 announcing a staff conversation in Singapore on April 18 composed of representatives from the United States, Australia, New Zealand, the United Kingdom, and the Netherlands East Indies. Its purpose was to prepare plans for the conduct of military operations in the Far East in accordance with *ABC-1*. Hart was directed to arrange transportation not only for his own representative but for the representative of General Grunert, but neither were to leave Manila until they had had time to study the *ABC-1* which was scheduled to arrive by courier by April 14. Special attention was invited to paragraph 31 of Annex 3. As previously stipulated, any agreements reached were subject to Stark's approval.[16]

Paragraph 31 of Annex 3 to *ABC-1* became, as Stark suspected, a seed of discord. It read:

> 31. In the Far East Area the responsibility for the strategic direction of naval forces of the Associated Powers, except of naval forces engaged in supporting the defense of the Philippines, will be assumed by the British Commander in Chief, China. The Commander in Chief, United States Asiatic Fleet, will be responsible for the direction of naval forces engaged in supporting the defense of the Philippines.[17]

The conference in Singapore lasted from April 21 to 27 with the United States represented by Captain Purnell, who by now was a familiar person at Far East conferences; Colonel A. C. McBridge, Assistant Chief of Staff, United States Military Forces, Philippines; Captain Archer Meredith Ruland Allen, the United States naval observer at Singapore; and his army counterpart, Lieutenant Colonel F. G. Brink. The British representatives were the ranking British officers in the Far East: Air Chief Marshall Sir Robert Brooke-Popham, Com-

mander in Chief, Far East, and Vice Admiral Sir Geoffrey Layton,
Commander in Chief, China. The ensuing ADB (American, Dutch,
and British) agreement reflected a decidedly British position, possibly
due to the influence of the much more senior British officers. The official *ADB Report* was not received in Washington until June 9; however, the British Military Mission in Washington received from London a telegraphic summary of the report and circulated it to the
American delegation on May 6.[18]

The information in the summary on the recommended defense
of the Philippines was the first major fault with the report. It
prompted the American military chiefs to inform the British military
mission of their reaction without waiting for the complete report.
Commander Lewis Richard McDowell, American secretary for col-
laboration to the British Joint Staff Mission, was instructed to inform
the British mission in Washington that the United States intended to
adhere to its earlier decision not to reinforce the Philippines except
in minor particulars, such as the addition of several minesweepers
and a few torpedo boats. The American military chiefs also believed
that the principal value of the position and strength of the United
States forces in the Philippines was in the fact that their defeat would
require a considerable effort by Japan and might well cause a delay in
the development of an attack against Singapore and the Netherlands
East Indies. A Japanese attack in the Philippines might thus offer opportunities to the Associated powers to inflict losses on Japanese naval
forces, and to improve their own dispositions for the defense of the
Malay Barrier. The Chief of Staff and the Chief of Naval Operations
did not agree that Hong Kong was likely to be altogether a strategic
liability, rather than an asset. They considered that Hong Kong, like
the Philippines, might contain or delay Japanese forces which would
otherwise be employed in a more decisive theater. As to the document
itself:

> . . . the Chief of Naval Operations and the Chief of Staff regret that
> they must reject this paper in its entirety, as either being contrary to
> the commitments of *ABC-1*, or as relating to matters which are the sole
> concern of the British Government.[19]

The dissatisfaction over the *ADB Report* registered in June with
the British military mission in Washington was just a preview of a
longer, stronger, and more detailed denunciation a month later, after
the American military staffs had had time to study the full report. A
joint letter from the Chief of Naval Operations and the Army Chief

of Staff directed the special naval and military observers in London to
inform the British chiefs of staff that the United States was unable
to approve the *ADB Report* for "several major, as well as numerous
minor particulars." The major objections may be summarized as fol-
lows:

(a)   Statements requiring political decisions were included in the re-
      port; specifically: that an attack on one of the Associated powers
      would be considered an attack on the other powers (paragraphs 6
      and 8); counterattacks on Japan would be recommended in the
      event of certain listed Japanese actions (para. 26); a call for in-
      creased assistance to China (para. 78).

(b)   The creation of a new intermediate command was not envisaged in
      ABC-1 The "Eastern Theater" and Commander in Chief, Far East-
      ern Fleet, had not been planned in *ABC-1*. The United States had
      agreed to British naval strategic direction of naval forces not en-
      gaged in the defense of the Philippines. There had been no agree-
      ment to the use of United States forces by the British outside the
      Far East area.

(c)   The strategic importance of the Netherlands East Indies was not
      appreciated.

(d)   After the arguments over the importance of the defense of Singa-
      pore during the *ABC-1* conversations and as a concession to British
      insistence in the final writing of the report, the following was in-
      cluded as part of paragraph 11(b): A permanent feature of British
      strategic Policy is the retention of a position in the Far East such
      as will insure the cohesion and security of the British Common-
      wealth and the maintenance of its war effort.[20]

In addition, paragraph 4 of the *ADB Report* had listed as the most
important interests in the Far East: (a) the security of sea communications and (b) the security of Singapore. Yet, in spite of the importance,
repeatedly stressed by the British, of the Malay Barrier to the security
of Singapore and the whole Far East, only three of forty-eight British
ships in the Far East were assigned to operate in the vicinity of the
Malay Barrier. No British vessels whatsoever were committed to the
naval defense of the barrier against Japanese naval forces advancing
southward, nor to offensive operations designed to close the barrier
to the passage of Japanese raiders. All British naval forces were assigned to escort and patrol work, most of them at great distances from
the position which the British chiefs of staff had asserted to be "vital."
It was pointed out that the naval defense of this position was en-
trusted, by the *ADB Report,* solely to United States and Dutch forces.
Since the eventual dispatch of a strong British fleet to the Far East

was considered problematical, the Chief of Naval Operations and the Chief of Staff advised the British chiefs of staff that, until such time as a plan was evolved whereby British naval forces could take a predominant part in the defense of the British position in the Far East area, they would be constrained to withdraw their agreement to permit the United States Asiatic Fleet to operate under British strategic direction in that area. The incongruity between the British position in Washington that Singapore was *sine qua non* to their Far Eastern security and the British position in Singapore of assigning none of their ships directly to support that theory was undoubtedly the major provocation for American rejection of the *ADB Report*.

(e) The assignment of United States naval aviation units to British control was in violatiin of paragraph 14(f) of *ABC-1*.

(f) There was no strategic plan in the *ADB Report*. Although American and Dutch forces had clearly defined tasks, those tasks assigned the British could "be approximately deduced only from the deployment proposed in Appendix 1."

The report was completely unacceptable to the American military chiefs. This instant failure, immediately following the concordance of strategic considerations in *ABC-1,* and the history of past failures to get the Far Eastern military commanders of the Associated powers to agree on a strategic plan of action against the Japanese, induced the Chief of Naval Operations and the Chief of Staff to suggest that if further conferences were to be held in Singapore for drawing up an operating plan for the Associated powers, that an agenda to guide the deliberations be agreed upon in advance.[21]

Before another Singapore meeting could be scheduled or the need arise for an agenda, the British chiefs of staff attempted, after the Atlantic Conference, to salvage the *ADB Report* by bringing it in line with *ABC-1*. During that conference between Roosevelt and Churchill in August their respective military leaders had gotten together to discuss the shortcomings of the *ADB Report*. Despite the British efforts on October 3 the revised report, designated *ADB-2,* was rejected by the Americans. The British mission in Washington was informed that the United States staff had given very careful study to the Admiralty's proposals for a new Far East area agreement, and whereas the proposals of *ADB-2* had met some of the American objections, the fundamental defects ' had not been eliminated. In fact, Admiral Turner thought that it not only was not an advance on the original report, but that it actually represented "a retrograde step."

Although neither the United States Army nor the Navy had reached a final decision, at the time they were inclined to believe that, until a really practicable combined plan could be evolved for the Far East area, it would be better to continue working under an agreement for coordination of effort by the system of mutual cooperation. The various commanders in the Far East were exchanging ideas and establishing technical procedures required for cooperation. Therefore, failure to issue a plan for unified command would not greatly retard progress. They felt quite strongly that the defense of the Malay Barrier was primarily a concern of the British and Dutch. Turner's suggestion was that the British chiefs of staff in London give this matter their earnest attention, and endeavor to prepare an effective campaign plan that would "have real teeth in it."[22]

Admiral Turner, in his letter rejecting *ADB-2,* mentioned to the British representative that "the military situation out there has changed considerably since last Spring, and will change more after the United States reenforcements, now planned, arrive in the Philippines." It was more than just planned reinforcements that changed the desperate strand of pessimism found in 1939 to 1940 to a fiber of hopefulness and, finally, restrained optimism. The dynamic personality of General Douglas MacArthur, recently recalled to active duty in command of United States Army Forces in the Far East; the mobilization and intensive training of native Philippine troops; the enthusiasm for the offensive power in the newly proven B-17 bombers which were to be flown to the Philippines in increasing numbers; and additional patrol planes, submarines, and torpedo boats for naval use in the Philippines all gave substance to the belief that within a few months the Philippines could be defended against a Japanese attack regardless of other agreements in the area.

While the United States was accelerating efforts to defend the Philippines, the British were re-examining their plans for defense of their interests in the Far East. Ghormley in London told Stark by dispatch on October 25 of a most important decision made by the British.

Admiral Tom Phillips, former vice chief, naval staff, was going at once direct to the Far East in *Prince of Wales* as Commander in Chief, Eastern Fleet, accompanied by Rear Admiral Arthur Francis Eric Pallister as chief of staff and additional staff officers. United States progress with *Rainbow 5* implementation and early repairs to British ships had enabled the Admiralty to plan an early dispatch of battleships to the Eastern Fleet, eventually to bring the total there to six;

however, they had only eight destroyers available of which four were modern.

The Admiralty felt that *ADB* was dead and that *ABC-1* was sound, and that what was needed was "a strategical operating plan" which could be drawn up in London or Washington but, better yet, in the Far East. Such a plan might require the use of Manila as an advance base for *ADB* naval forces and the development of adequate air routes throughout the area for concentrating of air forces. The Admiralty believed the disadvantages of the proximity of Manila to Formosa and possible effective air attacks had been disproved in the European theater. It was apparent that the British were taking prompt steps to meet the Japanese threat by sending able officers to the theater of possible operations, by desiring to make sound strategic plans, and by reinforcing their naval forces in the Far East. Those forces, however, were deficient in destroyers, submarines, and strategically located secure bases.[23]

Ghormley's informal message to Stark was soon followed by an official letter from the First Sea Lord, Admiral Pound. Reiterating the gist of Ghormley's message, Pound stated that he considered that neither *ADB-1* nor *ADB-2* met the new conditions caused by a change of government in Japan. (General Tojo had become prime minister and home minister on October 17 while retaining his post as minister of war.) Pound suggested that the need for a conference to draw up strategic operating plans for the Far East based "afresh on *ABC-1*" had become urgent. If Stark agreed in principle to the abandoning of further discussions on *ADB-1* and *ADB-2,* and to holding a fresh conference on the basis of *ABC-1,* they could then proceed to discuss the agenda.[24]

Admiral Stark replied the next day, November 6, through Ghormley. He agreed that the United Kingdom and the United States should act promptly on Pound's idea. He then gave a hasty review of what the United States was doing in the Far East. The Army was reinforcing both land and air forces as rapidly as practicable and was training the Philippine Army intensively. The Navy was reinforcing the Asiatic Fleet with twelve modern submarines, eight of which had departed Hawaii on October 24 and the remainder on November 4. Six motor torpedo boats had been delivered to Manila and six more might be sent. Stark then shifted to a discussion of strategy. He believed that *ADB* should not be revived since *ABC-1* was an adequate major directive, which "should be implemented by a sound strategical operating plan drawn up between British, Dutch and United States Navies